The Balanced Teacher Path

How to
Teach, Live, and Be Happy

Justin Ashley

free spirit
PUBLISHING®

Library of Congress Cataloging-in-Publication Data

Names: Ashley, Justin, 1985–

Title: The balanced teacher path : how to teach, live, and be happy / Justin Ashley.

Description: Minneapolis MN : Free Spirit Publishing, 2017. | Includes bibliographical references and index.

Identifiers: LCCN 2016048376 (print) | LCCN 2016049560 (ebook) | ISBN 9781631981012 (paperback) | ISBN 1631981013 (paperback) | ISBN 9781631981654 (Web PDF) | ISBN 9781631981661 (ePub)

Subjects: LCSH: Teachers. | Work-life balance. | BISAC: EDUCATION / Professional Development.

Classification: LCC LB1775 .A725 2017 (print) | LCC LB1775 (ebook) | DDC 371.1—dc23

LC record available at https://lccn.loc.gov/2016048376

Edited by Brian Farrey-Latz

Cover and interior design by Colleen Rollins/Emily Dyer

Cover apple photo © Astrug | Dreamstime.com

10 9 8 7 6 5 4 3 2

Printed in the United States of America

Free Spirit Publishing Inc.

6325 Sandburg Road, Suite 100

Minneapolis, MN 55427-3674

(612) 338-2068

help4kids@freespirit.com

www.freespirit.com

FSC
www.fsc.org
MIX
Paper from
responsible sources
FSC® C005010

TO MY WIFE, SAMANTHA

When I was out of breath, you carried me forward.
When I fell on my face, you lifted me up.
When I turned away, you nudged me in the right direction.

I'm grateful for your love, faith, and strength.
I could never walk this path without you.

Note: While based on real people, the names of students and teachers have been changed to protect their identities.

Contents

The Balanced Teacher Path

When I was a senior in high school, I was living in poverty and just trying to make sense out of my circumstances. My parents had recently divorced. My sister and I were torn by it. My family was scraping by month to month, paycheck to paycheck, struggling at times for groceries and other necessities.

At school, I was the shortest boy in class, pimply faced, with a mouth full of braces. Teasing and bullying happened daily. And like all seniors, I couldn't help but worry about the future. *I'm seventeen now. I'll be out of school this time next year. What am I going to become?*

I felt limited. Boxed in. There weren't a lot of options for a poor teen working as a fry boy at a fast-food restaurant after school to make ends meet. I contemplated working my way up the ranks to become a store manager. But one day in between classes, my school counselor stopped me in the hallway and pulled me into her office. She told me about the North Carolina Teaching Fellows Scholarship—a fund that would completely cover the cost of college, as long as I committed to teaching for four years after graduation.

Earlier that semester, I had taken a Teacher Cadet class—an elective course where students assist an elementary schoolteacher—and really enjoyed connecting with kids. So I was definitely interested in teaching. But my chances of getting the scholarship seemed slim. My counselor explained that thousands of high school students applied each year, and only a few hundred would win the honor.

I didn't feel as though I could stand out in any way. It was like a Hail Mary play, but I decided to go for it. I wrote the required essay and mailed it in with the application, joining a long line of candidates vying for this chance.

A few weeks went by, and I still hadn't heard anything back. I had nearly forgotten about it. But then I walked to my mailbox and saw a letter addressed to me from Raleigh. I ripped it open and read:

"Congratulations, Justin. You have been awarded a full scholarship to a North Carolina University of your choice."

I will never forget that moment, reading the letter with tears of joy flowing down my face. I felt as though I was getting a new start. No more fry boy. I was going to get out of my hometown, change the world, and become a teacher.

Fast forward to the first day of summer in 2015. After several years of teaching in North Carolina—starting in elementary education and eventually moving to middle school—I was checking into rehab for depression and a prescription-drug addiction.

Wait, what? So much for changing the world. It felt like the end for me. What had happened?

The End

The students had left for the summer. My room was packed up. It felt empty. The back wall was lined with my students' desks. Their textbooks were stacked in a corner, towering like a Manhattan high rise. In the front of my room, the whiteboard still reeked of dry-erase marker. The board itself was clean. Snow-white. Empty. A blank slate.

My mind, however, was busy creating a list of reasons to quit and never return.

For seven years, I was in love with the job. Whatever It Takes was my mantra. I gave kids my everything. On Saturdays and Sundays, I came up with killer class projects and graded papers by hand. From Mondays to Fridays, I taught my heart out. To my principal, I was known as the *yes* man.

"Mr. Ashley, can you lead the Faculty Advisory Committee?" *Yes.*

"Mr. Ashley, can you coach the Odyssey of the Mind team?" *Yes.*

"Mr. Ashley, can you present at the staff meeting next week?" *Yes. Yes. Absolutely yes!*

By all appearances, I was on the path to being the Perfect Teacher. I made positive phone calls to the parents of my students every month and replied to email messages each workday. I even made home visits for conferences and tutoring sessions.

These people needed me. I couldn't let them down. So I ran when they called for help. I ran like an Olympian sprinting for the gold. The cheers in the crowd encouraged me to keep running. My class earned high test scores. My principal gave me "distinguished" ratings. My students were featured in newspapers and on TV. And I was given a few trophies: Rookie Teacher of the Year in 2008, District Teacher of the Year in 2011, and North Carolina Teacher of the Year in 2013.

This may all seem glorious, but all that glitters is not gold. That's why after seven years of running, I found myself slumped over in a rolling chair, contemplating throwing in the towel for good.

While I was winning as a teacher, I was losing in every other field. I'd devoted so much time to being the Perfect Teacher, I hadn't noticed that other parts of my life were falling apart. My marriage was in trouble, I was nearly a stranger to my son, and, after paying bills, I had less than $100 in my bank account. To top it off, I had become hooked on prescription pills: amphetamines and antianxiety meds each day, with a heavy-duty sleep aid each night. For a long time, I didn't see it. But I slowly came to the conclusion that the problems in my personal life were rooted in my unflinching commitment to my work life.

So by summer 2015, I was in my classroom making a list of all the reasons I should quit my job. I didn't want to quit teaching, but I didn't want to teach anymore either. I didn't know what to do. I grabbed my workbag and drove home.

I found my house to be a lot like my classroom—mostly empty and silent. My wife and son were out for the evening. I was completely alone. It was clear that something had to change. *I* had to change.

So what does a lonely, dead-broke, burned-out, pill-popping Teacher of the Year do on the last day of school? He checks into rehab. My wife left work early; we talked it over and agreed on a plan for recovery. Not long after, I voluntarily enrolled in a nearby rehab facility.

"What's your profession?" the nurse in the front office asked me as we filled out the paperwork.

"Teaching . . . for now."

It took seven years of sprinting for me to discover that the Perfect Teacher Path can contribute to self-destruction. This was not at all how I pictured my life going.

The Problem with the Perfect Teacher Path

Teachers are nurturers by nature. It's part of our programming. It's instinctive to help everyone: students, parents, principals, and fellow teachers. We think that if we can effectively solve others' problems, we're doing the right thing. If we can just close the achievement gap, if 90 percent of our students will just meet growth, if our principal will just approve of us, then we'll be perfect. Whatever It Takes. But there is one problem: This mindset that serves our students so well has the power to drive us to burnout, to extinguish the fire for teaching. This is an issue for many of us.

Burnout can happen to anyone, and the signs can sneak up on you. Maybe you've got several years of teaching under your belt, and lately you hear yourself snapping at students for petty offenses. Or maybe as soon as your principal starts talking in the staff meeting, you assume more bad news: *What are they going to dump on us now?*

Or you might be a new teacher, and your creative juices are running dry prematurely. Coming up with fresh ideas for lesson plans is already feeling overwhelming. And with so many papers to grade, you skip writing real feedback and instead give participation grades.

You are pulled in so many directions: planning, assessing, teaching, learning, and responding. It's hard not to feel helpless, as though there isn't enough—material, time, technology, or support—to do your job effectively.

Many teachers feel burnout. The warning signs listed above are just a few. Fortunately, this doesn't have to be our experience. There is a way to teach and still be happy. It's a secret path, one far less traveled. I was lucky enough to stumble across it while I was in rehab.

The Life-Changing Lesson I Learned in Rehab

I started the summer of 2015 with an all-inclusive, four-night, five-day vacation in rehab. That definitely hadn't been part of my original plan for the Perfect Teacher Path.

Throughout the week, I received great treatment from the staff. The nurses made sure I had clean clothes to wear and good food to eat. The counselors listened patiently while I explained my career, family, and medical history. The doctors ran diagnostic tests and reviewed reports with me in great detail. The staff made me comfortable during my stay, but they didn't teach me the lesson that changed my life. That lesson came from another patient. I didn't even get her name.

She was young—in her late teens or early twenties—and yet she taught me such a wise, profound lesson. For teachers, the greatest lessons can come from the humblest of places. It happened during a breakout session in the main meeting room. I was seated in a circle with other patients. We were doing introductions and sharing a few personal tidbits with the group. One by one, patients were asked to give their names and share one thing—one accomplishment—that made them proud.

> Teaching is one element of who you are, but it's not everything.

First, a golf club manager told us about his rise to the top of his industry. Then, a landscaping business owner told us he was proud for starting his own business. After that, a guy who was the first person in his family to earn a doctorate degree shared his story.

Then, the young woman spoke up. I tried not to stare at the bandages over the cut marks on her arm as she gave her name. With a strong sense of conviction, she said:

"I am student. I go to school. I also work a job. But more than anything, I am a mom. *I am a mom.* A proud one. I've heard a lot of people talk about their jobs and successes in their careers. I am not rich. I am not a boss. But I am a mom. More than anything, that's who I am, and that's what I'm proud of."

I am a mom. Something within me clicked when I heard that. When trying to decide what to share about myself with the group, I hadn't even thought about my son or my wife. My only instinct had been to talk about teaching. After a few minutes, it was my turn to speak. I cleared my throat and said, "I was going to introduce myself as Justin, an American history teacher and North Carolina Teacher of the Year, but the Mom of the Year changed my perception."

I raised my voice boldly as she had and continued, "I am Justin. I am a proud father and husband."

As the people in the circle continued speaking, my thoughts drifted back. I was starting, finally, to make sense of my troubled past. It became so clear. Since my first day of teaching, my identity had been completely wrapped up in the teacher persona. *Mr. Ashley*. But what about *Justin*? What about *Husband*? What about *Daddy*? What about my health? What about me?

And that's what I learned. It's the lesson of a lifetime for a teacher: Teaching is one element of who you are, but it's not everything. You can be a good teacher, even a great teacher, but you don't have to be a perfect teacher. This was the end of the Perfect Teacher Path for me. If I was going back into teaching, I was going to do it on my terms and no one else's.

Balance. That would be my new focus: the Balanced Teacher Path.

The Balanced Teacher Path

Since I've returned to the classroom, I've discovered the difference between the two paths. The Perfect Teacher Path is about miles-per-hour, but the Balanced Teacher Path is about symmetry, not speed. Sprinting, or even jogging, is the wrong strategy. It takes a walking pace, a careful rhythm, as if you are crossing a balance beam. You can't run across recklessly at full speed. If you do, you'll lose control and fall. But if you move slowly and strategically, it can be done.

What does this approach look like in practice? At the parent meeting? At the dinner table? On Sunday afternoon? Or on Monday morning?

A Balanced Teacher looks at the bigger picture. A Balanced Teacher pursues happiness, not perfection, in every area of life and not just one. A Balanced Teacher:

- says *no* to the wrong opportunities at school
- says *yes* to weekend dinners with friends
- takes trips with family or friends
- avoids conflict in the workplace
- lives below his or her monthly wage
- makes learning fun every day at school
- accepts feedback from the principal
- communicates to parents with a quiet confidence
- takes her or his own recess after school
- plans dream work weeks

The Benefits of the Balanced Teacher Path

This even-keeled approach to teaching doesn't benefit just you. It helps those in your inner circle, too. Your friends, family, and coworkers. And, of course, your students.

When compared to the Perfect Teacher Path, the Balanced Teacher Path allows you to protect your passion and affect more students in a deeper way, over a longer span of time. You won't burn out. You'll be happier and healthier. And you'll last longer.

You can walk this path. You deserve this path. Your chosen career shouldn't leave you feeling stressed, overwhelmed, or depressed. If this is where you are right now, the good news is you can take a detour. Life is too short. This job can be exciting. The journey can be enjoyable and meaningful, but the first step is to stop the sprint.

In the chapters that follow, I'll walk you through ideas that have helped me find equilibrium. We'll look at changes I made—big and small—that you might make as well to bring balance to four key areas of your life: social, career, physical/emotional, and financial. I genuinely hope my experience helps you start along the path to your own balance.

Remember Lao Tzu's words of wisdom: "A journey of a thousand miles begins with a single step."

Let's start with that first step.

Part One

SOCIAL HAPPINESS

For those who don't guard against it, teaching can create an unwelcome sense of isolation or solitude.

Weekend schoolwork steals time away from our families. A low salary limits our budgets for shopping trips and outings with friends. And while we're teaching at school, we're physically trapped in the classroom as the only adult in a room full of kids.

Summertime is a different story. You don't have to read test papers (as long as you don't teach summer school). You have more opportunities to relax. Time, more often than not, can feel endless.

Until summer's end. That's when time speeds up, and before you know it, you're back in your classroom.

Social Happiness is about building, or rebuilding, a network of connections with the people in your life—your spouse, children, friends, fellow teachers, boss, and students. This diverse crew can cheer you on, push you forward, and pull you up when you're feeling down. So it's important to keep those connections healthy.

It's natural to let the high demands of teaching dictate your social life. But if you put energy into opening the door, inviting people in, and breaking out of your room, you'll find yourself on the way to achieving the balance you need.

Chapter 1

Be Wonder Woman, Not Superman

I remember watching the movie *Freedom Writers* in my college dorm room. As a teacher in training, I wanted to be just like Ms. Gruwell, the main character in the movie. Through grit and ingenuity, she transformed a seemingly unteachable group of poverty-stricken high schoolers into a devoted class with a hopeful future.

To do this, she threw herself into her job. She took a second job to buy classroom supplies, took her class on a field trip to Washington, D.C., and put in long nights reading and grading her students' diary entries. Even though her husband left her because she worked so much, she transformed the lives of her students. She saved them.

When I was assigned my first class, I tried to be like Ms. Gruwell. I showed up to school early. I stayed late. I tutored kids after school. I called parents each month with updates about their child's progress. I volunteered to lead a club because no other teacher would. I took my kids to Washington, D.C. Everyone at school saw me as a superhero, but I was being a villain to my family and myself. I was miserable and exhausted, but I believed I was saving my students, and that was all that mattered until Jan, my faculty mentor, stopped me as I was power walking down the hallway.

Alarmed by the look on my face, she asked me what was wrong. I told her I didn't have time to talk and needed to get back to my room immediately. She stepped in front of me and pressed further, "You're not going anywhere until you tell me what's wrong."

I gazed down while trying to hold back tears. Then I rattled off a dozen things I needed to do before the day's end. "I've got a field trip to plan, a club to lead, parent phone calls to make, and kids to tutor—"

Before I could finish spewing it all out, she stopped me. "How do you feel right now?" she asked.

I paused, wiped my eyes, and looked up at her. "Overwhelmed . . . really, really overwhelmed," I replied.

"So next time someone asks you to do something, remember the way you're feeling right now, and instead of saying yes, respectfully tell them no."

> Be respectful to everyone who asks, but say no to the nonessential tasks that don't align with your priority list.

Looking back, her advice was certainly a game changer for me. But in the beginning, it wasn't easy to say no, even after the pep talk in the hallway. Teachers have an innate desire to help others. Heroism is in our blood. We need to save the world from ignorance and destruction. We need to fly to every student, parent, principal, and peer that yells for help. And in the beginning of our careers, at least, we think we can help them all, just like Superman.

You might feel the same urge, this desire to be Superman at school. Though we can't kill the instinct, we can satisfy it by being a different superhero altogether. Instead of Superman, be Wonder Woman.

Wonder Woman is a natural role model for teachers. Look at everything she can do:

- She flies an invisible airplane and can travel undetected.
- She has a golden Lasso of Truth that forces anyone in its grips to be completely honest.
- She can easily run sixty miles per hour.
- She can pick up objects as heavy as 50,000 pounds.
- She can stop bullets with her bracelets.

Wonder Woman has only one weakness: chains. If chains are welded onto her bracelets, she loses her powers. She can be rendered powerless by the objects that protect her. It's the same for teachers. We can use our power or give it away, based on our commitments. For teachers, overcommitment is the chain that binds us.

If we overcommit, if we try to do too much at school and do whatever it takes so that all kids learn, we can't accomplish anything. We will lose our superpowers. To be a Wonder Woman Teacher, we can tell some people yes, but we will have to say no to others. By doing this, we keep our hands free. This seems counterintuitive, but we need to prioritize ourselves first. Putting ourselves first is not selfish. By doing so, we equip ourselves to be more giving to those in our network—students, peers, friends, and family members. It's about saying no to select situations. That's the hardest part: making sure we choose which battles to fight and which ones to walk away from. Here are a few strategies that might help.

Spend Most of Your Time on the Things That Matter Most

Peter Bregman, author of *18 Minutes: Find Your Focus, Master Distraction, and Get the Right Things Done,* suggests a technique that I've found helpful: determine your top priorities and spend 95 percent of your time on them.

I listed my key priorities on a large, bright sticky note and taped it on the inside front cover of my planner. It serves as a reminder when I'm planning out each day. Grab a sticky note and try it. Of course, your list might vary from mine. These are some of my examples:

- Be happy and healthy.
- Be a loving, dedicated husband and father by spending time with my family.
- Make learning enjoyable and meaningful for students.
- Spend quality time with my closest friends.
- Act in accordance to my faith.

When a mother asks me about tutoring her son on Sundays, I pass on it because spending time with my family is higher on the list. When another teacher asks me to help start an after-school club, I decline because I wouldn't be able to work out at the gym.

My priority list is a constant gauge that differentiates between the *great* and *good* ways to spend my twenty-four hours each day. After you make your own list, post it where you'll see it: in your planner, on your refrigerator at home, on your desk at work, on your phone, or in a desktop file on your computer.

Be respectful to everyone who asks, but say no to the nonessential tasks that don't align with your priority list. I'm not saying you have to say no to everything, but stick to doing the things that interest you and say no to the ones that don't. This will disappoint some people: administrators, students, parents, and other teachers. You will receive eye rolls, sighs, and condescending emails. But you'll serve these people better in the long run if you're not exhausted from overextension.

In *Essentialism: The Disciplined Pursuit of Less*, Greg McKeown points out that while turning someone down is uncomfortable in that moment, it creates a more comfortable future. Many teachers cave in and say yes under pressure, but once they make the commitment, they will more than likely regret it later. By selectively saying no and enduring the temporary discomfort that goes along with it, your chances of avoiding overextension are much improved.

Quit One Thing

Here's another strategy to try: Identify three activities you do each week that eat up a chunk of your time, things that you could quit doing right now. These activities could be a committee role, a weekly quiz you grade, or an after-school club you volunteer for. When you've got three picked out, eliminate one of them.

By saying no to just one thing, no matter how small it is, you are changing your mindset from Superman to Wonder Woman, from Whatever It Takes to What I'm Capable and Willing to Do. You're quitting one thing so you don't burn out trying to do everything.

The Superman teacher rarely lasts long in the classroom. What *Freedom Writers* doesn't tell you is that Ms. Gruwell quit teaching after five years. There is only one type of superhero who lasts in the classroom: It's Wonder Woman. Protect your superpowers. Don't overcommit. Don't get chained up trying to be everything to everyone. Save yourself so that you can continue fighting for yourself and your inner circle.

Chapter 2

Get a BTF at Work

At just eighteen years old, Shawn Achor faced his first life or death situation.

In his book, *The Happiness Advantage*, Shawn describes how he was trapped in the fire maze of a burning building while training with other new firefighters. The goal of the exercise was to rescue a dummy trapped in the maze and escape the fire as quickly as possible.

Just as he had been taught, Shawn locked one hand with a firefighter who was holding the wall. He used the other hand to feel for the dummy through the dark smoke.

After searching for several minutes, Shawn knew his tank was running out of oxygen. In a last-ditch effort to complete the task, he let go of his partner's hand and crawled around the maze, searching for a way out. He never found an exit, but the veteran firefighters carried him (and the other newbies) out before it was too late.

> It's instinctive to run from others when we feel trapped, but our best bet is to hold on tight to the people around us.

Once they had all caught their breath, the trainers let the new guys in on the secret: There was no dummy in the building. They had been set up to fail.

Still, Shawn admits he learned a valuable lesson that day. It's instinctive to run from others when we feel trapped, but our best bet is to hold on tight to the people around us.

Teachers get caught off-guard and feel pressure, too. Like when our principal tells us she is going to pop in for a formal observation within twenty-four hours. Or when we scan our way down the grading spreadsheet and only see numbers that are closer to our students' ages than a passing percentage.

Like the firefighters in training, one response when the pressure starts to build might be separation. We barricade ourselves in our classrooms and try to come up with solutions ourselves, rather than reaching out and opening up to other teachers. We give up quality time with friends and family on the weekends to knock out more paperwork. We work harder. We work longer. We get tougher. We tell ourselves that if we continue to crawl through the smoke, we'll find our own way out of the maze. We're wrong, of course.

The Best Teacher Friend Solution

It's hard for us to make it through adversity if we try to do so alone. For most of us, the best way to get through the teacher struggle is to connect with other teachers. Hold on to someone you can talk to, someone you can trust to help you find a way through your problems. Try to find at least one person to count on who is more important than just a fellow teacher or a casual friend. They're the best of both: a Best Teacher Friend (or BTF, for short).

Can a friend at work really help? Absolutely, says a Gallup study referenced in *Wellbeing*, a book by Tom Rath and Jim Harter. Of all the participants surveyed in the study, those with a best friend at work were seven times more likely to be engaged in their jobs. Seven times! They were also more successful at engaging customers and producing higher quality work, and they had a higher level of well-being than solitary workers.

> The Gallup study found the number of employees who had a best friend at work was a mere 30 percent. Less than a third of the participants knew the benefits of having a close friend at work.

Maybe you don't have a BTF at school right now. Or maybe you are close with another teacher, but you've never really viewed the relationship as a friendship. Or maybe there isn't a teacher on your team that meshes well with your style of teaching. But a BTF doesn't have to be someone from your grade level, subject area, or even your school. You might feel a stronger connection with a teacher at a district training session or a teacher from a different system who lives in your neighborhood.

Whatever the case, find a BTF who shares your outlook. Don't be afraid to look high and low to find someone. Be picky about finding them. Look for these four qualities—competence, optimism, confidentiality, and honesty—before you let them into your inner circle.

1. COMPETENCE

BTFs don't have to win National Teacher of the Year, but they do need to be competent. They need to have a practical knowledge about curriculum, instruction, and assessment, along with an understanding of student discipline and management basics.

They need to know what differentiation is. They need to know about IEPs and 504 plans. To listen and chat, you need to be able to speak the same language: teacher talk. You can create a lasting teacher friendship incrementally and gradually over a long period of time, but you have to begin with a similar vocabulary.

2. OPTIMISM

Carol Dweck, a researcher and psychology professor at Stanford, outlines two opposing self-concepts in her book *Mindset: The New Psychology of Success.* One perspective, what she calls a *growth mindset,* is a belief that one's talents and abilities can be developed through persistence and hard work. People with this perspective have the ability and desire to grow. They're hopeful about the future. People with a *fixed mindset* are the opposite. They tend to be pessimistic about their ability to change their circumstances.

Growth-minded teachers pay attention and participate in professional development sessions. They experiment with different lessons and teaching styles in their rooms. They're genuinely positive when they talk about their kids. They seem passionate about their jobs.

Attitudes have a tendency to rub off on others, so surrounding yourself with positive people is a plus. And when looking for optimism, don't forget to shine the light on yourself. Try to be the positivity that someone else needs. It will make *you* a better BTF.

3. CONFIDENTIALITY

I remember getting to know a new teacher I worked with a few years ago. As we spent more time together, I began picking up on a pattern in our conversations. She always had something negative to say about another teacher in the school. Each time I spoke with her, she found a way to bring up the latest drama.

While I listened to her again talk about another teacher, I thought to myself, *If she's spreading this gossip about others to me, what gossip about me is she spreading to others?* After that, I began limiting my time with her to school meetings and mandatory work functions.

BTFs are confidants you can trust with the information you don't want published in the school newsletter. You can trust them with things you don't want discussed in the teachers' lounge, like constructive feedback from your principal or a complaint from a parent. You can share your struggle with them, and they won't share it with others. When you talk to them about a coworker or situation that's bothering you, they will keep it quiet and help you sort through it. They'll listen and advise.

4. HONESTY

According to Andy Andrews, motivational speaker and author of *The Noticer*, a friend is not someone who just accepts you for who you are: this person challenges you and pushes you to reach a higher standard.

I remember getting my student growth scores back after my first year teaching eighth grade. For the first time in a long time, my students didn't meet their expected growth. My scores were in the red. I vented to my BTF in the hallway, and he didn't hold back on his views. He pointed out a few areas where I could grow, namely using more consistent grading practices and teaching a stronger review unit before the final exams. It was an uncomfortable conversation; he called me out. I'm not going to lie—it stung a bit in the moment. It wasn't what I wanted to hear, but I needed it.

I worked to incorporate his feedback into my lesson plans. In a single year, my student test scores went from low growth to high growth, from one side of the spectrum to the

> A BTF is a confidant you can trust with the information you don't want to be published in the school newsletter.

other. The spike in scores wouldn't have happened if my BTF hadn't pushed me to do better.

Best Teacher Friends can be real with you. Hearing the truth may be difficult at first, but trust them and know that their intentions are good.

Keep Your Fire

As we learned earlier through Shawn's story, getting out of a burning building can be very challenging for a firefighter. But for teachers, our struggle isn't escaping the fire; it's keeping it.

> Our struggle isn't escaping the fire; it's keeping it.

We begin teaching with a fire in our hearts, but sometimes it comes close to being extinguished: the stinging feedback from a principal, the self-imposed guilt caused by a failing student, the words of condemnation from a parent that we rewind and replay in our mind, over and over again. It's moments like these that steal our fire.

If, for whatever reason, you feel your fire dying down, BTFs can help. They have a fire, too. One they're happy to share with you.

Chapter 3

Avoid Vampire Teacher Attacks

Most teachers you work with will be like you: driven, passionate, and hopeful, despite the limiting circumstances. But there probably are also Vampire Teachers lurking around you, too. There are a few in every school. At first glance, they look like typical teachers. But in reality, their passion for teaching is dying. Their negativity can feel like a bite that drains you of your own enthusiasm.

A few years ago, I read about energy vampires in *The Energy Bus* by Jon Gordon. According to Gordon, energy vampires are people whose sour attitudes can leech hope and drive (not blood) from the people around them. I thought the term was silly, but then I noticed an energy vampire in the hallway at school. And I ran into another one during a staff meeting. I started seeing them everywhere. It was only natural to make the leap from *energy vampire* to *vampire teacher*.

> At first glance, Vampire Teachers look like typical teachers. But in reality, their passion for teaching is dying.

What exactly does a Vampire Teacher look like? And how can you protect yourself when one attacks? Read this survival guide. Commit it to heart. It could save your career, even your life.

Vampire Teacher Survival Guide

Table of Contents

1. Identify potential vampire teachers in your environment.

2. Avoid confirmed vampire teachers as often as possible.

3. If you become exposed, smile before they bite.

4. If you are attacked, find energy donors immediately.

1. IDENTIFY POTENTIAL VAMPIRE TEACHERS

Spotting Vampire Teachers can be tricky at first. If you suspect someone of being a Vampire Teacher, use recent encounters with the teacher in question as a baseline to answer the following questions:

- Is he the first to deliver gossip about his peers in the teachers' lounge?
- Does she ask for more help from her fellow teachers than she gives in return?
- Does he talk about his students' weaknesses more than their strengths?
- Do her students seem less happy in her classroom than they are in others?
- Does he have higher expectations of others than he has of himself?
- Does she resist school changes more often than she embraces them?
- Do you feel more pessimistic about your job after talking with him?

If you answered yes to any of these questions, you might be in danger. Proceed with caution.

2. AVOID CONFIRMED VAMPIRE TEACHERS

The best weapon against a Vampire Teacher is avoidance. Stay away when you can. If you must be in close proximity, avoid direct contact. In meetings, surround yourself with BTFs on the other side of the room from where the Vampire Teacher is sitting. On the playground, don't engage the Vampire Teacher in conversation. During bus duty, talk with the bus driver or teachers who are more upbeat. Be covert and cordial about this. Stay polite to everyone in the environment, but be strategic about who you let into your inner circle.

3. IF EXPOSED, SMILE BEFORE THEY BITE

You may find yourself cornered in a room. A Vampire Teacher pulls up a seat right beside you in a meeting. Or maybe you get paired with a Vampire Teacher by your principal for a professional development session.

Protect yourself when you get stuck. If you can't change the environment you're in, change the discussion. Lead the direction of the conversation. Speak first, before the Vampire Teacher starts complaining. Compliment the other person's outfit or talk about something that excites you.

The content of the discussion matters less than the direction. Simply start by being positive. Get the Vampire Teacher smiling, maybe even laughing. This could inject hope and protect you from losing your joy while in the other person's presence.

4. FIND ENERGY DONORS IF ATTACKED

Negativity spreads quickly and easily. Words from a Vampire Teacher have the power to alter your mood for the whole day. After you're exposed, try surrounding yourself with energy donors—teachers, parents, students, and support staff—who lift your spirits and remind you of why you teach. Energy donors can help you refuel.

Beware of the Internal Vampire

Let's pause for a moment of introspection: while there may be Vampire Teachers around you, it's important to recognize if there's also one within you.

Have you felt discouraged a lot lately? Have you been complaining to others? Have you made sarcastic jokes or harsh judgments about students, parents, teachers, or your principal? It's healthy to wrestle with the idea that you could be a Vampire Teacher. I'll admit that, for a few years before I found balance, I was one. By changing my behavior outside of school, I was able to improve my attitude inside school. When I took control of my personal relationships, physical health, diet, and finances, things started turning around. If you find yourself burning out from teaching, continue seeking balance—this could help you reenergize. The internal vampire probably won't disappear immediately, but it is likely to get a little quieter each day until it eventually becomes silent.

Another tactic is to be an observer. Look around in the hallway and teachers' lounge for genuinely happy teachers—those who smile and make others smile a lot. What do they say? What do they do? Replicate it in your own way. There's nothing wrong with being a copycat.

It's better than being a vampire.

Chapter 4

Connect with Kids

Helen Keller faced several significant challenges to learning as a child living in the late 1800s. She was deaf, blind, and mute. As a young kid, she would lash out at her parents and teachers, screaming and crying in frustration. Who could blame her? Helen couldn't understand anyone, and no one could understand her.

But that all changed through the help of one teacher: Anne Sullivan. At just twenty years old, Anne had a breakthrough moment with Helen. She took Helen to an outdoor water pump and flushed water into one hand, while spelling the word *water* in the other hand. It worked. For the first time in Helen's life, she connected a word with a physical object.

Anne continued using this kinesthetic method to teach Helen. Within a few months, Helen had learned almost 600 words, the majority of her multiplication tables, and how to read braille. Anne didn't stop helping Helen, even as she got older. When Helen began attending Radcliffe College in 1900, Anne used sign language to translate the lectures and helped Helen break down textbook vocabulary. A few years later, Helen Keller became the first deaf-blind person in the world to graduate from college.

Whenever I read about this story, I can't help but think about this fact: Helen was able to succeed as a student because of the connection she had with her teacher. On a very personal level, Anne did what no one else could do. She communicated with Helen in a format that made sense. Not through sound or sight, but by touch. As teachers, it's critical for us to connect with our kids, not just to teach content but also to show them we care.

The experience of childhood can become more distant with time. The older we get, the more difficult it can be to relate to kids' experiences and problems. We need to see the world through their eyes and communicate through a filter that makes sense to them, no matter how foreign it may seem to us.

The Student-Teacher Relationship Is Fundamental

We spend more time with kids than we do with our peers, principal, or students' parents. For most of our day, we are surrounded by kids. So it makes sense that, out of everyone we work with at school, having healthy relationships with our kids is the most essential. Children are more likely to meet expectations when the student-teacher connection is strong. It can improve our influence and effectiveness throughout the school year.

> For kids, this formula often proves itself true: $r + r - r = R$ (rules plus responsibilities, minus relationship, equals Rebellion).

How Can We Connect?

Our students come to us with various backgrounds, cultures, and socio-economic statuses. They come with different preferences for connecting. Gary Chapman highlights several examples in his book *The Five Love Languages of Children*. Some kids feel a bond when they receive encouragement, others by spending quality time with an adult. While one student builds a bond when she plays soccer with a teacher outside, another feels connected when her teacher praises her for her improvement in math class.

As teachers, we need a toolbox of strategies—ways to connect with kids, no matter the circumstances. Here are a few ideas that have worked for me. Some of the tips can be done with the whole class; others can be used on a student-by-student basis.

POINT OUT STUDENTS' SUCCESSES WITH COMPLIMENT SLIPS

Leave sticky notes on students' desks after school, celebrating something they did right, no matter how minuscule it may seem. Maybe a student's re-test was five points higher than the original. Or maybe a student was walking in line quietly and ignored another kid acting out. Even if students aren't succeeding in big ways, point out that they already are in small ways. Consistently pointing out small successes may lead to larger ones. Just make sure the praise is genuine. Find real things to praise. Empty praise isn't helpful in the end.

Angela Watson has some phenomenal sentence starters and compliment slip templates for a very reasonable price at unshakeablebook.com.

JOIN STUDENT TEAMS AT RECESS

Join in with kids as they play games they love. Whether it's basketball, soccer, or tag, they will feel more connected to you if you share an experience they enjoy.

A few years ago, I remember feeling frustrated with Daniel, a student in my fourth-grade class. He would rarely talk to me when I called on him in class or when I had to reprimand him for bad behavior. He wasn't completing his classwork or homework. And almost every day in class, students would tell me he was using words that no ten-year-old should understand.

About a month into the school year, I saw him playing two-hand touch football with a few other boys at recess. I ran over and asked him if I could play all-time quarterback. I discovered Daniel was fast, faster than all the other boys playing. I started throwing him pass after pass. He caught each one. He would sometimes get tagged after running for a few yards, and other times he would run the ball for a touchdown, followed by a Cam Newton–style touchdown dance. When we were walking back to school, I pulled him aside and told him how impressed I was with his catches and lightning speed.

For the rest of the school day, it was as if I had a new student in my class. The old Daniel had become a new boy. He raised his hand and asked questions about the lesson. I didn't get any reports about foul language. From then on, I played football with Daniel as often as I could. His behavior going forward wasn't always perfect, but the connection we made helped us avoid major problems the rest of the school year.

JOIN KIDS FOR LUNCH

One or two days a week, I like to opt out of lunch in the teachers' lounge. Try it for yourself: Sit and eat with your kids. Turn lunchtime into quality get-to-know-you time. Start with general questions and follow up with more probing questions that require more than one-word answers. If you ask about a student's weekend and find out he or she went to the movies, start a discussion about favorite movies and the funniest moments on the big screen. Lunchtime conversations can help you and your students discover that you have a lot more in common than you thought before.

ADD KIDS' PASSIONS TO YOUR LESSON PLANS

Our curriculum, what we teach, is nonnegotiable. There's no autonomy for you to change the curriculum for your students. We have to teach what we teach. For example, a U.S. history teacher has to cover the Civil War. But the instruction, *how* we teach the Civil War, can be adapted based on your teaching style and the needs of your kids. Find out what your students love and mix it into your lessons.

Crystal, a student in my eighth-grade class, was obsessed with Nirvana. Images of Kurt Cobain covered her T-shirts. I used this fact when it came time to learn about the Gettysburg Address in class. We compared the speech to the lyrics of Nirvana's hit song "Come as You Are" and looked for similar themes. Crystal was grinning from ear to ear when she walked up to me after the lesson and asked, "Mr. Ashley, you picked that song just for me, didn't you?"

It's all about relationships.

"Of course!" I responded.

If one of your kids shows you pictures of his Maltese at home, figure out how to incorporate dogs into a writing activity or an interactive read-aloud. If another student wears a basketball jersey to school every week, teach statistics using her three-pointer completion percentage and average assists per game. The more you get to know each student and incorporate that knowledge into your lessons, the more likely it is you'll find a connection.

LET STUDENTS LEAD APPRECIATION DAYS

Kids who enjoy acts of service typically like giving them just as much as receiving them. Set up class service projects each year and have a few students lead the effort to help others in the community and building. On top of service projects, consider organizing student-led appreciation days to honor school staff.

When I taught elementary school, my class sponsored a Janitor Day and Lunch Lady Day one year. The kids in charge came up with all kinds of ideas to recognize our undervalued staff members at our school. They presented thank-you cards, goody bags, and roses to each worker. One lunch lady began crying after a student hugged her and handed her a flower. She told us that even though she had worked in the cafeteria for over fifteen years, no one had ever thanked her for doing her job. The act of service was an opportunity for us to fill and feel fulfilled at the same time.

KNOW WHEN TO TEACH AND WHEN TO CONNECT

Random opportunities to teach life lessons sometimes come along throughout the school year. When this happens, I've found I have to stray from the learning objective and planned lesson to own the moment.

About halfway through last school year, I received a phone call from another teacher on a Saturday. He broke the news that an eighth grader in my homeroom, an easygoing boy named Jason, had died in a car accident. With my teacher peers and students, we went to Jason's funeral on Monday. Then Tuesday came, and it was time for class—without Jason. Time to teach. To read. To talk history. Time to move on. But I wasn't ready for that. And my kids weren't either.

All I could do was stare at his empty desk. It was one chair over from the door to our room. He was just there last week. A few kids were crying. Some were staring down at their desks. Others were staring at me, waiting for me to break the silence. I held back my tears and admitted to them that I wasn't ready to move on either. I told them that even though Jason was gone, he would always be a part of our lives. He would always be a part of our classroom.

I reached in my bag and grabbed a handful of colorful sharpies. I handed them out and gave my students permission to graffiti his desk: funny things he said, symbols of his hobbies, and words and phrases that described his personality. They drew skateboards, a violin, and his Boy Scout sash. In the very center of his desk, they rewrote the caption from his final post on social media a few days before the car crash. He had taken a picture of the ocean with the sun in the distance and, almost prophetically, said "Together, we can face any challenge as deep as the ocean and as high as the sky."

To this day, Jason's desk still sits as a permanent memorial in my old classroom. When former students come back to visit, they sometimes stop and take pictures, even stare at it, smiling as they remember who he was and what he stood for.

As a class, we drew closer together in an almost unimaginable way. That's what it took to power through the tragedy. I hope you never lose a student. But throughout your career, there will be moments that can't be anticipated, chances to teach something beyond the test. Don't be afraid to stray from the lesson plan. Open up. Be vulnerable. Connect with students on a personal level.

All teachers care about their kids, and the most effective teachers show they care in ways their students can understand. This may take thinking out of the box. It's unorthodox. It's like what Anne did with Helen. She saw life through Helen's lens, where Helen couldn't see or hear. But she could feel.

Communicate to Parents with Confidence

Chapter 5

This isn't awkward. This isn't awkward. This isn't awkward.

I kept lying to myself while holding a transparency of male genitalia. Seventy sweaty fifth-grade boys were staring at me as I stood at the front of my classroom. I was mentally preparing myself for a lesson I was required to teach about sex education. Specifically, the male reproductive system.

For the lesson introduction, I addressed the elephant in the room. "Boys, I expect you to be mature in our lesson today, as this is information you need to know. But I also know that this is an unusual topic, so I'm going to say the word we are all thinking, and then you can get your giggles out for ten seconds. After that, we will get serious. Deal?"

They nodded their heads in agreement.

"Okay," I said, "the word is . . . penis." They busted out laughing while I counted to ten.

For the next thirty minutes, they followed through on their end of the deal. I walked them through the parts and functions of the male reproductive system. After that, we viewed a videotape (yes, it was that old) that explained puberty. The most awkward part was the end of the video, when a cartoon image of two penises flashed together on the screen, one unstimulated and one erect. Semen shot out of the erect penis into a vagina while the narrator described how babies are made. After that, the screen went black. Just like that, it was over. I had officially survived the weirdest lesson ever. Or so I'd thought.

After school, I was called down to the office for a parent phone call. "This mom seems really angry," the secretary warned as she handed me the phone. I was terrified. I didn't want to answer. I took the phone with hesitation. The mother on the other end said, "What did you teach my son in school today? He's been crying since he got home from school because he thinks he's supposed to have two penises, and he only has one!"

After catching my breath, I quickly explained the ending to the video we had watched in class. We both laughed it off, and she apologized for jumping to conclusions. The experience really taught me something about teacher-parent communication: there will often be gaps between what students experience at school and how they explain it to their parents at home.

> There will often be gaps between what students experience at school and how they explain it to their parents at home.

This does not necessarily mean that the teacher, parent, or even the student is to blame. Sometimes it's like the telephone game. As the original message is whispered from one person to the next, it changes slightly with each iteration. The ending of the game provides the best lesson for teachers: always check with the source of the message to find out what was really said.

Speaking with a parent about his or her child can be intimidating. But you don't need to begin any conversation fearfully. Before you return a call, sit down for a meeting, or respond to a parent email, try these three things so you can respond with confidence.

1. Be Prepared

A few years ago, I found myself at a teacher appreciation ceremony, waiting to receive an award on my school's behalf. Before the event started, I saw the host backstage, standing near a wall . . . and she was talking to it! I was weirded out at first, but then I realized what she was doing. She was running through her speech, making hand gestures as she paced back and forth, pretending the wall was the audience that awaited her. Later, when she walked on stage to deliver her real speech, it was flawless. The crowd was fully engaged.

If you practice what you are going to say before you say it, you'll be more comfortable when the spotlight is on you. Briefly in your mind, or even out loud, you can rehearse explanations or responses that may arise in the parent conversation before you actually have it. Preparing your responses can really calm your nerves when you are in front of an audience or a parent.

It's also helpful to gather evidence, with as many tangible details as possible, before you respond. If you are calling about misbehavior, do you have written notes from the incident? Did you talk to other students who saw what happened? If you are calling about academics, have you looked for patterns or outliers in grades from previous weeks, grading periods, or even school years? Have you talked to the student's previous teachers? Do you have work samples handy in case you need them for reference? Tangible evidence and testimonies from others can help you make your case if necessary.

It's also important to establish well-defined boundaries. Parents should know that if they cross these lines, you will end the call or face-to-face meeting. You earned a college degree. You studied. You passed your tests. You observed. You student taught. You applied and your school could have picked many candidates, but they picked you to be the teacher. You deserve to be treated as a professional. You have the right to end any conversation with a parent who curses, screams, or threatens you.

When a parent crosses any of these lines, future communication will need to take place in the presence of an administrator. Let the parent know you no longer feel comfortable speaking privately. Right after the meeting ends, let your principal know what happened and how you responded. If you can't find the principal on campus, send her an email and save it, in case you need it at a later point for reference.

To be honest, it's impractical to think a teacher can be completely prepared for every encounter. A parent might stop you at a random moment in the hallway on your way out the door. Or you might get a frantic phone message from the father of your best student. Even if you have no idea what's coming, you can act as if you do. Stay calm. Stay in control. Not just with your words, but also your body language. If you feel attacked, don't cross your arms. Just listen intently and take a deep breath before responding. You have no say in how the situation arises, but by staying at peace, you remain in control of your emotions and increase the odds of working toward a solution.

2. Be Coachable

The teacher-parent team is a lot like a head coach and an assistant coach. But one key difference is that teacher-parent roles are interchangeable through the season. It's more like co-coaching, where either person can take the lead. In the academic arena, for example, teachers take the lead. We're the experts. But in the field of discipline or behavior, parents may possess a better skill set, at least for their child. Why is that? Because they have more plays in their playbook. They have observed their child from birth. We have less than a year of our own observations to bank on, but a parent has witnessed several seasons of play.

If the strategies and interventions you are using in class aren't working, let down your guard and ask the parent for ideas. Try asking questions such as "Is there something you do at home that I can try here at school?" or "Is there a strategy that worked better with last year's teacher?" Ask parents to open up their playbooks and you may find a way to apply it in the future. Be coachable. This gesture scores big with parents because it shows them you care more about helping their children than about being in charge.

3. Be the Dinner Conversation

I have often heard the advice, as you may have, to start off the beginning of every school year with a positive call home to a parent of every student on the class roster. It's a great idea, but the first few weeks of school are among the busiest, often jam-packed with meetings, paperwork, and setting up routines. You might be reluctant to call parents at night from home. You might decide it's better to recharge by jogging around the neighborhood, getting lost in a new hit novel, or binge watching an online show. But even with this bit of self-care, you know it's important to keep those channels of communication open.

While calling every parent may be difficult, there is a way to connect without a voice call. It's not by texting. You can communicate with parents indirectly, through the conversations they have with their kids. On the ride home from school or sitting around the dinner table, most parents often ask their children questions like "What did you learn today?" or "How was school today?" Your connection travels through their answers to those very questions.

One of the greatest compliments I have ever received came from a single dad at a curriculum night event just a few weeks after the school year started. After I finished my presentation on the curriculum units and student projects for the year, the dad walked up to me and introduced himself. He continued by saying that his son, Gabriel, hadn't talked about school at home in previous years. Gabriel had faked being sick on multiple occasions to try to stay home. After school let out each day, he would run to his dad's car and pretty much stay quiet the whole ride home.

But this school year, the dad went on, was different. Since the second week of school, Gabriel was waking himself up and getting ready on his own so that he could get to class on time. At the dinner table each night, he was talking about the fun projects he was doing in school. Rather than counting down the days to Saturday at home, he was now counting down the days to Monday at school.

The best way to connect with parents is to create a learning environment that is both meaningful and pleasurable for their kids. Giving a student the motivation to come to school and providing them with an experience worth talking about at home creates not only a conversation, but a line of trust, respect, and honor between the most influential people in a child's education: parents and teachers.

> The best way to connect with parents is to create a learning environment that is both meaningful and pleasurable for their kids.

If I could take a time machine back to when I answered that angry parent phone call, I would tell my past self, *What could this parent say to you that's worse than talking to ten-year-olds about penises and vaginas? You made it through teaching sex education, and you'll make it through this phone call, too.*

You survive so much adversity each school day. You keep your cool when your printer runs out of ink. You find the right words to say when a student is crying in despair. And you manage to piece together your lesson plans with little time and only a few resources. If you are strong enough for all of that, you can answer a parent's question with a confident voice, not a trembling one.

Chapter 6

Swallow Feedback from Your Principal

Like a fish swimming upstream, I tried making my way through the body of students rushing down the hallway. The students were power walking to their homerooms. I was jogging to my car, already late for a district meeting off campus. Before I could leave, I had to drop off my sub plans to Mrs. Lewis, the assistant principal, in the front office. I was still trying to catch my breath when I finally made it to her doorway. I stood there while she comfortably sat behind her desk, sipping her coffee and checking emails.

"Here are the sub plans you asked for," I reminded her.

Mrs. Lewis gazed through my papers, paused, and looked back up at her computer. "These plans aren't detailed enough, Justin. You can do better."

Her words were a punch in the gut. My face turned red. I took a step toward her desk and flipped out: "I'm so sorry you feel that my plans aren't enough, but I think they are more than enough. And just so you know, I stayed up until two o'clock this morning doing schoolwork, including the plans you're holding in your hand right now. I think you could be better . . . better at pointing out my strengths instead of just my weaknesses." I stormed out of her office, ran to my car, and sped off to my meeting.

On the long drive there, I replayed the scene in my head, trying to make sense out of what happened. Eventually, I freeze-framed when it all went wrong. It began the split second after I heard my principal's feedback: I choked on it. Rather than chew and swallow, I chose to spit it back in her face.

The Problem with Feedback

I hope you never go off on your boss the way I did. Even though my response was unusual, the frustration with feedback is common. Usually, the most discouraging part of a principal's feedback isn't the feedback itself; it's the way the feedback is delivered that gets us fired up.

It might be delivered at the wrong location: "Did he really just call me out in front of my peers in a team meeting? Why not meet me in my room for a one-on-one?"

Or it could be delivered at the wrong time: "It's Friday. I've worked sixty hours this week. I'm exhausted. And all I get is an email reminder that he still needs my paperwork from last week."

Or it's delivered by the wrong person: "I hardly even know her. She's half my age. She's a brand new principal who's only seen me teach for three minutes in a walk-through. What does she know?"

It's easy for us to dismiss what was said because of when and where we received it and who we received it from. That's what I did when I rejected my boss's advice. It was too early in the morning. I was too tired from working late the night before. And I was too late for my meeting to process anything negative, so I refused it. I choked on it. But choking every time you eat only means you will starve to death. A good teacher who wants to become great takes feedback, chews on it, and swallows.

If you want to benefit from what I learned the hard way, here's my advice: Every time you get feedback from your principal, or your mentor or supervisor, approach it as if you are dining at a restaurant. The people giving feedback are the restaurant owners, cooks, and servers. You are dining in. Get the most out of the meal.

Understand the Food on the Menu

In my principal's office, I had expected her to serve me up a steak, medium-well . . . something like, "Thanks for staying up late to do these fantastic substitute plans." Instead, she gave me a you-can-do-better salad. It wasn't the response I was hungry for. But the feedback we refuse to swallow is often the feedback we really need to eat.

In Thanks for the Feedback, Harvard lecturers Douglas Stone and Sheila Heen suggest identifying the feedback before you try to process it. They cite three types: appreciation (thank you for doing that), coaching (instead of doing that, do this next time), and evaluation (this is where you stand with me right now). We need each type of feedback to grow throughout the school year. Receiving affirmation like "That teaching strategy was so creative" or "I really appreciate you stepping up to lead the Girls on the Run club after school" could really lift your spirits. There are other times when you just need a solution, such as when you are completely out of ideas on how to help a student or how to collaborate with an abrasive teacher across the hall.

It's ultimately up to principals to give the just-right dose of feedback. That's no easy chore because they have to do this for *every* teacher. So it's probably best not to be picky. Whatever we are served, let's take it in and do something with it. Let's be grateful for it. Even if it is not what we crave in that moment, it is what they feel we need.

> The feedback we refuse to swallow is often the feedback we really need to eat.

No matter the dish they serve, we can use each type to our advantage: Appreciation reminds us we are making a difference in the lives of our kids. Coaching helps us become better at teaching. Evaluation gives us an expert's assessment of where we stand. To help you swallow the dish that's being offered, ask yourself these questions:

- What type of feedback am I expecting from my principal? Appreciation? Coaching? Evaluation?
- What type of feedback is my principal giving to me? Appreciation? Coaching? Evaluation?
- Do I need to realign my expectations?

If the conversation is not what you expected, get on the same page so you can see the feedback for what it is.

Change How You Chew

The way you eat salmon is different from the way you eat an ice cream cone. One food necessitates a knife and fork; the other requires repetitive licking. Similarly, receiving feedback requires a specific response, depending on how it's delivered.

If your principal is coaching you, asking for clarification will help you get on the same page. To avoid sounding bossy, your principal might offer feedback as hints or subtle suggestions for improvement, rather than direct advice. For example, if your principal begins a post-observation conference by advising you to make your lessons more rigorous and relevant, asking questions will help you discover more:

o Can you describe a lesson you have observed recently that was both rigorous and relevant?

o What specific parts of the lesson seemed to be too simple?

o When I plan my lessons for next week, how could I do a better job of challenging my kids with the content I'm teaching?

To the receiver, coaching advice can seem vague. There's a difference between what is stated and what we infer. Ask your principal clarifying questions. This encourages explicit communication of expectations. And it's empowering for you to understand exactly what to do when you walk out of your principal's office.

Evaluation, unlike coaching, tells you where you rank in the present. You could be evaluated on student learning outcomes, parent communication, or classroom management. Evaluative statements usually take place at the end of each school year in your final conference with an administrator.

To get the most out of an evaluation, view the judgment from two distinctive lenses: present and future. Think to yourself or ask your principal questions such as these:

o What does this say about me right now? How should I respond? How does this measure up with former feedback I've received?

o What will change for me next school year? Will I be given more responsibility to my grade level team? Will I have less flexibility in how I plan?

> It's true that we don't always have the power to make the right choices, but we can usually make our wrong choices right.

Remember: an evaluation is really just a chance to see your performance through your principal's eyes.

The third form of feedback, appreciation, is what we usually love to hear. It's the sweet stuff. It could be a shout-out at a staff or team meeting. Or it could be a compliment your principal passes on to you after a parent raved about your class.

In some schools, principals rely more on coaching and evaluation, but appreciation is just as important. If you are fortunate enough to get positive feedback, try to extend it beyond that moment. Write it down or, if it's in paper form, like a thank-you card or an email, print it out and hang it up somewhere in your room so you can remember what was said.

If the Food Looks Bad, Get a Second Opinion

You wouldn't bite into a piece of moldy bread or undercooked chicken. Questionable advice is no different. If it doesn't feel right, get a second opinion.

Talk to your BTF—someone you can trust to be honest. Start with something like "This is how my principal told me I should have handled the situation differently. I really feel like I did the right thing. What do you think?"

In some cases, you will realize you were just overreacting and needed an unbiased viewpoint to bring you back to reality. Other times, you may find that there is some truth to your gut feeling. If this is the case, try following up with the administrator and ask for clarification.

Commit to Doing One Thing

Figuring out what to do with feedback can be difficult. It's natural to feel offended, disappointed, or overwhelmed when facing constructive criticism, but try not to get tangled up with the emotions. Instead, think about one thing you can do with the feedback immediately after the meeting or conversation.

It could be something simple, such as including at least one informational text into your instruction each day. Whatever it is, give your principal a verbal commitment—*This is what I'm hearing from you. This is what I am going to do today and tomorrow.* You may not be able to decipher and fix everything all at once, but you can do at least one thing. And that's all it takes to show your boss that his or her feedback didn't fall on deaf ears.

A few days after the incident with my sub plans, I realized how problematic my response to the assistant principal really was. I started thinking back to the conversations we'd had over the years—in the hallway, at the media center, on the bus lot, in my classroom, and in her office. I remembered the moments where she sang my praises and recognized me for my creativity.

I realized that in the times where she had coached or evaluated me, she wasn't really evaluating me as a person; she was just telling me where I stood or how I could become better. But when I snapped in her office, I screwed up by taking a professional conversation very personally. I didn't chew. I didn't swallow. I choked under the pressure.

After realizing my error, I apologized. My assistant principal could have disciplined me, but she forgave me instead. And since receiving her advice, I've put together two- to three-page sub plans with detailed instructions and activities for every school day I've missed. As Andy Andrews points out in *The Traveler's Gift*, it's true that we don't always have the power to make the right choices, but we can usually make our wrong choices right.

Receiving feedback can be a humbling experience. It takes hard work to process feedback in a positive way. It takes humility and selflessness. But consider this—teachers who chew on their principal's words can also swallow and digest the advice, allowing the teacher to be healthier, happier, and more effective in the classroom. On the flip side, teachers who choke on the feedback they need could end up starving to death while waiting for the food they desire.

Chapter 7

Follow a Weekend Plan

Can you imagine teaching without a lesson plan? Picture a teacher in front of a room full of students with no learning objective, no materials prepared, and no activities planned. What would be the outcome of such a lesson?

The teacher would fumble around the room trying to come up with an activity for the students to do. Kids would begin doodling on papers and putting their heads down on their desks in despair. Every second that passed would feel like an hour. Students wouldn't learn anything, because there was nothing to experience.

The Problem with Freestyle Weekends

We would never go through a lesson without a plan. So why do we go into each weekend without one?

In my first year teaching, I hated plans. My entire workweek was dominated by them: lesson plans, 504 plans, and IEP plans. The last thing I wanted to do when I left school for the week was follow another plan. I went home each Friday craving sleep like a bear in winter. I needed to hibernate. So that's usually what I did. I slept in late on Saturday and Sunday mornings. I took naps in the afternoons. I ran a few errands and graded a few papers when I could. But mostly, I slept. That's what

I thought my body needed following a busy week at school: rest. After a few months of this weekend pattern of constant sleep, I noticed a paradox: I was more tired each Monday morning than I was the Friday before.

I've learned a lot about weekend planning from Laura Vanderkam's book *What the Most Successful People Do on the Weekends*. Mostly, I've learned to view Saturdays and Sundays as more of a reward to be enjoyed rather than a time to fall asleep. After spilling blood, sweat, and tears at school each week, part of a teacher's weekend could be spent at rest, but a lot of it can be spent awake and feeling truly alive.

> To make a weekend plan, use an index card or a piece of paper; print out the free template at justinfashley.com; or make a copy of page 138.

Don't get me wrong. I'm not suggesting that anyone should spend every waking moment of the weekend at play. The laundry pile would grow as big as Mount Rushmore in just a few weeks' time. While there are chores and repairs that need attention, the trick is to compartmentalize and maximize your time for more enjoyable tasks. Sketch out a weekend plan, a modification of the lesson plan you use at school. It only takes a few minutes to complete each Friday night or Saturday morning. It doesn't need to be thorough, just organized. Here's what mine often looks like.

OBJECTIVE

I always start with an objective, two weekend goals at the top of the page:

1. Enjoy the weekend.

2. Recharge for the workweek.

SCHEDULE

Next, I flesh out what needs to happen. When doing this, intermix your must-do's and get-to-do's. Your must-do's are chores, such as washing dishes. And get-to-do's are fun things, such as going to the movies with a friend.

My schedule sometimes looks like this:

TIME	ACTIVITY
Friday night	arcade with Cole
Saturday morning	wash, dry, and fold laundry
Saturday afternoon	work out at boxing gym
Saturday night	watch movie with fam
Sunday morning	go to church
Sunday afternoon	grade unit tests, finish lesson plans
Sunday night	pick up groceries/toiletries for week

It's likely that your must-do and get-to-do lists will vary each weekend—one weekend might include filing taxes or car repairs, but during the next weekend, you somehow squeeze in a workout, manicure, and pedicure all before lunch on Saturday. The focus here is not hitting a specific number of things to do. It's about habitually maximizing your weekend time at the end of each week.

If, after a few months, you begin to notice you're overwhelmed with things you must do on the weekends, stop and analyze each part of your schedule. What can you say no to? What can you cut out? Is every must-do really a must?

ASSESSMENT

We test students with pop quizzes to assess if what we're doing in class is working. To make sure your weekend plan is working, test yourself with a three-question assessment, due to yourself each Monday morning. You can go over the answers in your head while getting ready in the morning or in the car on your way to school.

1. How do I feel when I look back on my weekend?

2. How do I feel about the week ahead?

3. Was my weekend with a plan more fulfilling than past weekends without one?

If your answers are positive, the plan is working!

One Last Thing—Don't Forget to Differentiate!

There is such a wide range of ability levels and learning styles in every classroom. Some students learn faster than others, some enjoy working in groups, and others prefer independent learning. We differentiate by varying the way we teach to best suit a student's needs. Our weekends should work in a similar fashion, with a variety of different kinds of get-to-do's:

o **Social versus solitary:** The weekend is the best time for friends and family. Be sure to connect with others, but also make time to withdraw: meditate, read, or write by yourself. Just you. Even if it's only for a few minutes each Friday night. Make time to be both a recluse and a social butterfly. Bounce back and forth from one to the other.

o **Outdoor versus indoor:** The simple act of exposing your skin to sunlight provides a spark in happiness. Try to do at least one thing outside every Saturday and Sunday, maybe a quick morning jog or a dinner out on the patio. Chores such as putting away laundry, unloading the dishwasher, and vacuuming the carpet will provide plenty of time indoors, so be more intentional about getting outdoors and getting some sun when weather allows.

> When coming up with activities, I've found that the balance of how much of each type of activity to pursue is up to the individual. Some people might need time alone to recharge, while others need a highly social environment. Do what feels best for you.

o **Physical versus mental:** You are not wasting minutes of your day when you curl dumbbells and sprint on the treadmill. You are adding years to your life expectancy, releasing endorphins in your brain, and stepping up your energy level for the days ahead. But just hitting the gym isn't enough. It's good to give your brain a workout, too. Try cooking a new recipe. Sit down and do a crossword puzzle. Join a book club at a local library. Listen to a TED Talk or take a free online training course. Go back and forth between stretching your body and mind, all weekend long.

Weekends aren't just about rest. They are also about rejuvenation. Stephen Covey's legendary career advice—begin with the end in mind—applies to the weekend, just as much as it does the workweek. By putting a plan on paper, you will get the most out of your days off. You won't just snooze through the weekend, you will experience it, learn from it, grow because of it, and, most of all, enjoy it.

Chapter 8

Take Family Field Trips

Weekend work comes with the job. We can't fully eliminate it, but we can periodically escape it and reduce the psychological impact it has on us. In short, we can manage it so that it doesn't consume the weekend.

The Best Escape from Weekend Schoolwork

A few years ago, I remember typing up lesson plans for the first week of school as the summer was coming to an end. My family was spending the last day of summer at play while I was trying to get ahead for work. My planning spot was on the dock of a lake. My wife was sunning herself beside me. My four-year-old son, Cole, was jumping around on a giant water tube, tied to the dock. To him, it wasn't a water tube. It was his pirate ship. He waved his sword around as he protected his treasure from an imaginary Captain Hook in the water.

Then he stopped abruptly. "Daddy," he begged, "can you stop working and play pirate ship with me?" He wanted me to join his crew.

"Not right now. Maybe later," I insisted. He frowned for a second and started playing again without me. I knew he meant well, but he was a distraction. I had too much prep work for school.

After an hour or so, I decided to take a break. I plugged my headphones into my phone and hit the play button on Laura Vanderkam's audiobook about enjoying your weekends. How fitting. Her first point hit me hard: We're not really living in the weekend when we spend it prepping for the workweek. The most successful people don't put off enjoying the weekend. They do it now.

I flashed back to what I had said to my son when he wanted to play. Then I thought, *Maybe not later—maybe now.* I turned off my phone and closed my laptop. I yelled out to my son as I ran toward him, "Captain Cole, look out for the cannonball!" His eyes were as wide as an owl's when I jumped off the dock and crashed into the water just beside him. When I came up with water spewing from my mouth, he was laughing uncontrollably. We spent the rest of the afternoon paddling around, fighting Captain Hook, and searching for gold doubloons.

Later that night, I finished listening to the audiobook. It offered a second tip that inspired me to continue resisting the temptation to work during future weekends: Plan fun events that get you out of the house and keep you busy. I've come to refer to them as Family Field Trips.

> Use the Family Field Trip Planner Template on page 141 or download it at justinfashley.com.

On the way home the next day, my wife and I wrote down a list of fifty places we could travel to as a family within a two-hour radius of our home. Some trips would last a few hours, but others could be an entire day. We started taking our Family Field Trips the next weekend, and we've been hitting the road pretty regularly ever since. We've visited the Transportation Museum. We've picked out dozens of books at the local library. We've stood under the waterfalls where part of *The Hunger Games* was filmed, sat in the front row at a college football game, and shoveled out handfuls of food to giddy llamas at the zoo.

Let's clarify *Family* in Family Field Trip. Please know that I use this term loosely. You might not be married with kids. Maybe your family is more extensive—your parents, a sibling who lives nearby, your cousins, or your current partner. Maybe your family is a handful of close friends who you love to hang out with. You love socializing and you are in your element when they are around. Or maybe *you* are your family. You're a proud introvert. You fly solo. Your dream day consists of reading a book by yourself on the beach. Your family is your inner circle. It doesn't matter who that consists of.

A Family Field Trip is more about the act of escaping. Breaking free. Going to a place where the work can't follow. I'm not saying the work just disappears into thin air. The school stuff is still there when you return. But if you occasionally work late on Friday nights or show up early every so often Monday mornings, you can look forward to your weekends instead of dreading them. When you return to school, you'll find yourself more efficient because you're well rested and not burned out.

Make a Family Field Trip List

By yourself or with your family, create a list of places where you want to travel. Try to come up with at least fifty places, each within a two-hour radius of your home. Setting a limit on the travel time saves you the added expense of an overnight hotel stay. Some of our most memorable trips have been free or cheap, such as when we broke the high-score record for a Skee-Ball game at an arcade or when we hiked the trails at a nature park.

Keep the Plan in a Highly Visible Location

Place your plan on the fridge or in the corner of your bathroom mirror. Put it anywhere in the house that works for you, so long as you'll see it often.

In *The Happiness Advantage,* Shawn Achor references a research study on positive psychology, where participants who just thought about watching a favorite movie raised their endorphin levels by 27 percent. Just by thinking about the movie. You can similarly lift your spirits simply by seeing your field trip list. It can remind you of a favorite trip you've taken before or one you are looking forward to.

Our list stays in our kitchen, just above our key box. Every time I drop my car keys off or pick them up during the week, I get excited about the family vacation that awaits.

Make Family Field Trips a Monthly Routine, Not an Occasion

Commit to a regular excursion, whether it's once a weekend or every month. The goal is not to take all fifty field trips in a year; it's to build a routine of spending time with your family. It's all about stopping to smell the roses so you can travel from Monday to Friday without running on empty.

To this day, my son will sometimes stop and remind me about our pirate excursion at the lake. He refers to it as "The Best Day Ever." It was as awesome for me as it was for him. And to think, it almost didn't happen because I wanted to get ahead on a few lesson plans.

Ultimately, your weekend belongs to you, not your principal, your district, your students, or their parents. Given the heavy workload you carry each week, you deserve a break. Don't let it get hijacked by your to-do list. Get out of your house or apartment. Lose yourself so the schoolwork can't follow. This is a transformative choice—for you and those around you.

Part Two

CAREER HAPPINESS

Career Happiness is not about the big picture. It's about zooming in on part of the picture. Your time, resources, and energy are all finite. Because of these limitations, it's all the more important not to take what we have for granted. Just like magnifying a picture on our phones, we've got to zoom in on what matters most at school. That's the key to being happy.

A recent study on mood changes confirms something you probably already know from experience: On Fridays, most employees become significantly happier than they are throughout the week. Why? It's the end of the workweek and the beginning of the weekend. This section is about making Mondays great and keeping your joy going all the way through Thursday. We shouldn't have to wait four days each week to be happier.

Chapter 9

Fail. Fail More. Succeed.

During my first year as a teacher, I was psyched for a new history lesson I'd planned to present to my third graders. I'd opted not to settle with the suggested lesson—reading from a textbook about the American Civil War. I didn't want my students to just read about a historical period in the past—I wanted to bring it to them in the present. To accomplish this goal, I decided to dress up as a Civil War soldier, surprise the students by jumping through an imaginary time machine (aka the classroom window), and explain what living in the 1860s was like. I called it the Past Blast experience.

I was so excited about it that I even invited Mrs. Summers, my literacy facilitator, to check it out on the big day. While she stayed with the students, I ran to the teachers' lounge to change into the wool costume. After I assembled the matching hat and beard, I bolted outside toward the open window of my classroom.

It was supposed to be a great lesson, but it was the worst one I've ever taught.

With sweat dripping from my arms, the moment I had been waiting for had finally arrived: the jump. But the jump through the window became more of a stumble when I tripped over the ledge. I hit the floor in my classroom with a thud. When I got back on my feet, I noticed the students were totally thrown off. A few were screaming and running toward the door, mistaking me for a creepy intruder who'd broken into the room. Others, who could see through the costume, just laughed out loud.

When I finally got the class settled down, I attempted to deliver a speech in character that discussed weaponry, rations, and key battles of the Civil War. I received no standing ovation after the performance, only silence as confused students looked around at one another and occasionally glanced up at the clock on the back wall. They had no idea, or interest, in what I was talking about. I hadn't thought to provide them with any background information about the Civil War before the Past Blast. It backfired.

Still, I continued. I handed out reading passages and questions about the Union and Confederate armies. That's when I found another flaw with my plan. The text difficulty level of the reading passages was way too high. Hands shot up throughout the room, asking for help. My facilitator and I rushed around, trying to explain the confusing words in the questions I'd posed. Some students tried to answer them, while others just doodled on their papers. I could see it in their eyes. They were all disappointed. I was, too.

I took questions at the end, making a last-ditch effort to connect with the kids. Every question they asked was either silly or completely off topic, revealing that they were more curious about my fake beard than they were about history.

It was supposed to be a great lesson, but it was the worst one I've ever taught. And it was the most humiliating moment I've ever experienced as a teacher. I failed. Big time. After I brought the lesson to a close and my facilitator quietly escaped the room, I took off the beard and wiped the sweat off my face. A little later, I dropped my students off at the bus lot, rushed back to my room, closed the door, and cried. I crumbled up the lesson plan that had taken hours to create and threw it away.

Then I took a step back to reflect. My Past Blast lesson was essentially a good idea. True, the execution of it was bad, but that didn't mean it had to be trashed. Why couldn't I make it great? In that moment of introspection, I felt this overwhelming urge to recycle the Past Blast lesson—not into the blue bin next to the trash can but into my plans for the next school year. So I retrieved the lesson, smoothed it out, and started writing down ideas that could improve the lesson. I continued doing the lesson, and every year I find ways to refine and improve the experience.

> If you're creative enough to think of a different way to teach, you're creative enough to look beyond your own failure and find a path to success.

Now in the weeks leading up to every Past Blast, each student compiles research and creates a trading card about the historical figures I've introduced before that character visits the class. They also turn in five questions they could ask. I choose a few of the best ones for the Q and A session with the character.

I also review rules about posture, eye contact, raising hands, and taking notes in interactive notebooks. This encourages structure and order so students can stay focused and learn during a lesson that's unusual.

The last change to the lesson was a major one. Rather than dress myself up, I bring in true historical experts: trained reenactors from local museums. Over the years, students have had the chance to meet World War II paratroopers, a Continental Army soldier from the Revolutionary War, and Katherine Wright (the Wright brothers' sister), to name a few. To top it off, my dad paid an artist to paint a time machine around the window for the reenactors to climb through as they journeyed into and out of the classroom.

At the end of each school year, students often cite Past Blasts as a highlight, one of their favorite lessons of the entire school year. But they never would have experienced any of them if I hadn't dug through the trash can after teaching my worst lesson. As teachers, I think we're quick to trash good ideas that go bad because they're embarrassing, but they can often be recycled into something greater. If you come up with an original instructional idea and it fails, treat it as a draft and not the final copy. Do what we teach our students to do in writing: reflect and revise, repeatedly.

If you're creative enough to think of a different way to teach, you're creative enough to look beyond your own failure and find a path to success. I know; that's easier said than done. It's extremely scary to jump through a window and try something different. It's even scarier to do it a second time when the memory of falling on your face is still fresh. It's frightening, but it's worth it.

Author John Maxwell calls this concept Failing Forward. Rather than constantly trying to succeed, we should use failure as a learning experience, an opportunity for growth. Maxwell offers a simple way to apply this idea: turn the focus from internal to external. Failing makes me feel terrible inside (internal). But I can use the lesson I've learned to do better for my next class (external). How much can your students next year benefit from turning a good idea (gone bad) into a great one?

Try the steps outlined on the next page. This is the method I used to turn my Past Blasts, and many other failures, into lessons that worked for my students and for me.

1. Pick an Idea That Involves a Passion

Even when I was a kid, I loved theatre. That's why I chose to dress up and play the part of a Civil War soldier. I wanted to teach my audience through a performance. For you, it may be music, sports, or painting. Whatever it is, integrate the thing you love into what you have to teach.

2. Invite a Friendly Critic

Ask someone you trust to observe the lesson and give an honest reaction to your work. This may be a facilitator, an administrator, or a teacher in another hall. Opening yourself up to criticism is scary, but an observer may have a solution to a problem you can't yet solve. It also shows that you're a teachable teacher. The rewards far outweigh the risks.

3. Jump Through the Window

Show your grit. Close your eyes and jump. After you get the lesson rolling, be prepared to be unprepared. Be prepared to be embarrassed. Be prepared for the fall. You will survive the lesson. You will teach another day.

4. Reflect Back on the Plan

After the lesson is over, try to sit down with whomever you've invited to observe your classroom to review it. Let this person be your adviser. If a face-to-face meeting isn't possible, ask your adviser to email you his or her thoughts on the class activity. Specifically, ask for what went right as well as what went wrong in the lesson. Using your adviser's feedback and your own introspection, write out what you should continue doing and pencil in what needs to be changed. File your updated copy away until next year.

5. Repeat the Lesson

Each time you reintroduce and revise the activity, you'll feel the improvement, even if it's just a little. Over time, the novice lesson will become a masterful one.

Because you showed the courage to repeat your failure, you'll gradually fail your way to success. But remember, happiness is not only found in success.

We have to figure out how to be at peace with our failures. Try recycling them. By doing so, you can look back at a later time and see that the mistakes didn't go to waste.

Chapter 10

Write Student Thank-You Cards

We've all had them in our classrooms: students who, even if they mean well, can't stop themselves from blurting out or talking to their peers while the rest of the class is paying attention. It drives us crazy!

A student's disruption is always a distraction, for both students trying to learn and for the teacher trying to teach. Over the years, I've tried so many strategies to solve the distraction problem, but I've only found one solution that works every time. It came to me in a moment of frustration with a student who chatted on and on, even when I asked him to stop. One girl beside him put her finger over her mouth and pointed up to me when the student kept talking, trying to redirect. I don't know if he didn't get enough sleep the night before or was having a bad morning, but he refused to quit interrupting. Finally, I moved him to the back of the room until I could figure out what to do next. As we moved from our class discussion to an independent reading assignment, I considered how I could best respond to the student's disrespect:

- ○ I could address him in front of the class and kick him out of the room.

- ○ I could write him up and send him to the office for in-school suspension.

- ○ I could give him silent lunch and call his mom after school.

I'd tried all three methods before and was ready to try one of them again, until I froze near the back of the room and looked around. I hadn't noticed it before, but all the students in the class were fully focused, working hard on the assignment just like I asked.

Wow, I thought, *I had let the one chatterbox in my room distract me from the thirty-one at full attention.* Rather than lose my cool at the one kid who was off task, I quietly asked him to work outside of the room. Then I sprinted straight over to my desk.

I shuffled past a few folders and found some old thank-you cards I had stuffed away. I grabbed a pen and started writing. I thought back to a student who was raising his hand in class, participating in the discussion, and working well with everyone around him. I told that boy how proud I was of him this year and how lucky I was to have him in my class. I told him how he made me a better teacher every day and that he had a great future ahead.

On my break, I wrote five more thank-you letters to other student leaders I could think of off the top of my head. By the time I handed them all out, my frustration from that one disruptive student had disappeared.

I'm not suggesting that we play favorites with the students who are the best behaved, but we do need to frequently put our focus in check. Are we seeing solutions or just problems in our classrooms? Are we letting the misbehavior of a few overshadow the excellence of the rest? The biggest problem with calling out a student isn't the distraction they cause for other students. It's the distraction they create in you. Deal with them quickly and turn your attention back to where it belongs: on the good stuff.

Keep a Fuel Folder

James was one of the students who received a thank-you card in class that day. His mom emailed me that night and said:

Mr. Ashley,

I wanted to tell you thank you for taking the time to write that note. My son was so proud and was excited to show it to me. He often feels pressured to compare himself to his older brother, who is an A honor roll student. I want him to be who he is: social, fun, sensitive, and smart. But often, he doesn't give himself the credit he should. So thank you—you have made a huge difference to him this year, and I am very appreciative of your time and energy toward our kids. You go the extra mile.

Thank you!

I'm sharing this mother's response with you not to toot my own horn, but because I want to highlight how powerful one note to a student can be. It took me a minute to write the thank-you note to James, but it made his entire day. And it made him so proud that he wanted to show it to his mom as soon as he got home from school.

I printed the mother's email and stored it in a paper folder with others I've received. When you receive similar notes, keep them in a digital or paper file and title it Fuel Folder. This is something that helps you chug along. Rereading the notes from others will remind you of the importance of the cards that come from your pen. This strengthens your momentum and motivation to keep writing.

> Keep track of who you're giving cards to and how often. Without giving false praise, be fair and make sure everyone gets acknowledged with a note at some point.

In your college courses and professional development sessions, you've probably seen a lot of strategies for managing classroom disruptions: giving clear, consistent consequences; building a relationship with the student; and contacting the parents. These are all solid tips for directly dealing with a child who is disruptive. But the inconvenient truth is that a kid still might act out, even after you use every trick in the book. Writing thank-you cards to cooperative students is taking an indirect, proactive approach. Not for the sake of the kid breaking the rules, but for those who are following them and also for you—their leader.

The classroom is a microcosm of your life, where you are given situations that are far from perfect. In life and in class, don't let the bad outshine the good. This is how you make the best out of any situation.

Chapter 11

Deal with Discipline Issues Quietly

She was only nine years old. Abby looked innocent, but she was guilty. I caught her in the act, with folded paper in hand. *I bet it's a love letter*, I thought while I casually strolled over to her desk at the back of the room.

"Do you know my policy on note passing in class?" I asked, raising my voice so the whole class could hear me.

"No, sir," she responded.

"I confiscate the note and read it out loud to the whole class." This was a bit strong, I know, but I was a new teacher and ignorant about more student-centered responses.

Abby took a deep breath and shook her head back and forth. "Mr. Ashley," she begged, "please don't read that letter. Please. Please. Please don't read it."

I cleared my throat with flamboyance as I turned toward the rest of the class. "This will be the last time I have to read one of these letters to all of you . . . because none of you will ever write one in this room again."

I picked up the letter and unfolded it slowly to build up the tension. It took me nearly a minute or so, since it had been folded eight times. With her hands clasped together in desperation, Abby tried to stop me one last time.

"Mr. Ashley, don't!" she screamed.

I took in a breath to read the first sentence. That's when I saw my name on the paper. I stopped myself, choosing instead to read it silently.

I think Mr. Ashley looks better in skinny pants than he does in regular ones. What do you think?

Ugh! It was a love letter—sort of—about me! I quickly refolded that letter eight times and slid it back to my secret admirer. With a shared look, Abby and I agreed that we'd never speak about it again. To this day, I don't know who was more embarrassed by the situation. That was the last time I ever threatened to embarrass a student. It was a wake-up call that publicly humiliating a student is never an appropriate form of discipline.

Don't Make Private Matters Public

There are individual misbehaviors in every classroom that require discipline. It's instinctual to use them to teach the whole class a lesson. But I've learned that correcting a student privately can often save the student, and teacher, from public humiliation.

That doesn't mean we ignore mischief. We just address it without making a scene. Maybe you see a kid playing around during group work. Or you catch a student cheating on a big test. Avoid losing your cool and embarrassing yourself as I did with the love letter. Here are a few ideas to make discipline a private matter.

PASS THE ENVELOPE

A neat trick I've used to deal with discipline quietly is outlined in *Making Good Teaching Great*, a book by Todd Whitaker and Annette Breaux. It's called Pass the Envelope. When a student misbehaves continually in class and you can't put an immediate stop to it, write the name of a BTF on an envelope, put a blank paper inside, and seal it. You will have previously told your friend that you might send a student on an imaginary errand to deliver the envelope if you need to remove that student from class with minimal distraction.

Ask the misbehaving student to help you out by delivering the envelope to the other teacher. When the student leaves the room, close the door and lock it. This requires the student to knock upon returning. When you hear the knock, open the door and meet the student in the hallway before he or she can reenter. Thank the student for helping you out, and then suggest there's a way to help even more: by making better choices than the ones he or she recently made.

USE PEER PRESSURE

Some students don't care what you think about their misbehavior. You can talk about how disappointed you are until you have no oxygen left to give, and they remain unchanged.

Instead of rattling on and on about your opinion, share real complaints (if you've received or overheard them) from other students: *Hey, Brandon. I had two students come up to me after class yesterday. They both told me that you were really off task in class. They said they couldn't focus on their work because you were making farting noises with your mouth and armpit. You may have thought it was funny, but they thought it was childish and it upset them. How can we fix this?*

Teachers can point out a student's immaturity a hundred times, and it doesn't sink in. That's because kids who cause problems in class do so to get attention from other kids. They want their peers to see them as the class clown or the cool kid. But if they hear what other kids really think and not just what the adults have to say, they may lose interest in the disruptive behavior.

You are a teacher, but you are also like a coach.

Some kids will remain unfazed, even after hearing what other students think. Or maybe the misbehavior isn't impacting other students, just you. Either way, see if this next technique helps. It's worked for me, both as a giver and a recipient.

TEACH KIDS TO MAKE THEIR HISTORY REPEAT ITSELF

I was diagnosed with ADHD after almost failing my freshman year of college. Even now, many years later, I sometimes have trouble keeping attention, finishing tasks, and turning things in on time. To cope with this disability, I talk with my ADHD counselor for an hour or so every month or two.

In each session we have together, I talk about my problems. I recently asked him, how could I possibly write a work-life balance book for teachers while raising two kids, supporting my wife, and teaching 200 teenagers?

My therapist responded to my question by reminding me of my past. "What about when you went to grad school? Granted, you just had one child then. But how did you manage to get your master's degree when you were married and had a kid?"

I explained how I had broken down my big class projects into small manageable pieces, which I'd knocked out one-by-one on Sunday afternoons. I'd made an extra effort to help my wife when I was around, and I wouldn't let my son go to bed without reading him at least two books, no matter how exhausted I was.

"Justin," he said, "you've been here before. It wasn't easy, but you made it work in grad school, and you can do it again. If you could do it then, why not now?" I was reminded that the busyness would be temporary and that, while I would have to make some sacrifices for a short period, I could keep my priorities in mind and be back to full balance in time.

Every session with my therapist ends up like this. I talk about my present struggle, and he talks about my past strengths. He's exercising an element of *Cognitive Behavior Therapy*—a common sense approach to problem solving that involves changing a pattern of thinking. He's helping me associate my past behaviors with my current problems, which empowers me to replicate solutions.

I've found that it can work for students, too. Don't stop after talking about their misbehavior. Point them to a time when they were successful. Maybe they spoke up for a friend who was being bullied, taught another student a reading strategy in class, or showed leadership skills in a school club. Draw parallels they can envision. Connect the dots between their past successes and future possibilities.

You are a teacher, but you are also like a coach. When players miss shots they really should have made, the worst thing you can do is yell in front of the entire team. Save yourself and them from the embarrassment. Discreetly call these students over to the sideline and encourage them to score next time the ball is in their hands. Be picky with what you say and how you say it. The quieter you speak, the deeper they listen. The deeper they listen, the more you can teach, which improves your effectiveness and happiness at school.

Chapter 12

Put a Purple Cow in Every Lesson Plan

Years ago, before my daughter was born, my wife would occasionally travel to New York for work. When she did, my son and I were on our own for dinner. The fast-food drive-through was our lifesaver. During our fifteen-minute drive on the backwoods roads of Waxhaw, North Carolina, we routinely passed a cow pasture.

The first time we drove by, I yelled to the backseat, "Look, Cole, cows!" He was awestruck. Only two years old at the time, he had seen pictures of cows in books and on TV, but this was the first time he'd seen real, live cows. I tried not to take my eyes off of the road, but I couldn't help glancing back to see his excitement. His smile was one of wonder. He couldn't contain his joy. "Moo!" he screamed at the top of his lungs. Then again. And again. Over and over until we were out of sight. He was amazed.

A few months later, when my wife was gone again, we took the same route to dinner. I pointed out the cows to Cole just as I did before, but something had changed. Just like before, I pointed toward the pasture and yelled back to him. His response? Silence. No screams of "Moo!" Not a smile. Nothing.

His change in behavior really got me thinking. It reminded me of *Purple Cow* by Seth Godin. In the introduction, Godin describes a similar experience he had with his son on a family vacation while driving through France. His kid was excited at first, but he was bored again after passing pastures for several miles. The new cows seemed just like the old ones and were no longer interesting. A purple cow though, he explained, would have sparked his son's interest.

This theme easily lends itself to the classroom. When a teacher presents a straightforward lesson to students, it's not always something to moo about. It's too predictable. It's been seen before. But when something special is added, that's when the teacher enjoys teaching and students love learning.

Far too often, we hear about including daily objectives and assessments in our lesson plans. What we don't talk about is the purple cow. Your principal may not require it, but you need to make it a requirement to yourself: place a purple cow—something different, fun, and unexpected—into each lesson you teach.

Happiness isn't just about being happier right now. It's about becoming more upbeat about the future. Planning with purple cows gives you something to look forward to each school day. And it gives you street cred with your kids. They will look forward to your class because you will constantly take them by surprise.

Assemble a Digital Board of Directors

Corporations generally have a board of directors—a team of expert lawyers, financial advisors, and major stockholders—who meet with the CEO as he or she makes decisions that affect the whole company. If you're having trouble going purple on your own, put together a digital board of directors: educators who share creative lesson plans online and point you in the right direction. Organize links to their work in one place online for quick access at school or home.

Create a list of leaders you know in the education field: famous teachers, trainers, bloggers, and teacher organizations. Many teacher leaders will have their own websites. See what sort of resources they might have available online. Here are a few I had on my list: *The Cornerstone* by Angela Watson, the Ron Clark Academy, Edutopia, Teaching Channel, and the Gilder Lehrman Institute of American History.

Once you've got the links, find a place to store them online. There are several websites that will do this. The one I use is symbaloo.com. At Symbaloo, you start by choosing a dashboard template, which will give you several rows of tiles. Paste a link from the websites you've researched into each tile. Symbaloo will display a thumbnail image that relates to the link. The service then bookmarks the website so you can access it, just by clicking on it. Treat the tiles like seats at your boardroom table. Fill the seats with advisors from your list so they're all in one place. Whenever you sit down to plan your lessons each week, consult your board of directors at Symbaloo. Check out their websites. Look for innovative ideas. Dig for instructional tips. It's easy to draw a blank when you are on your own; researching other innovators can be a spark for your own creativity.

Here are a few examples of the purple cow at work, based on my students' favorite lessons and ones I've heard about from other teachers.

GAMING—WHAT GAME OR APP RELATES TO THE CONTENT I'M TEACHING?

Learning about westward migration can be dull, unless you're the one trying to survive the 2,000-mile trek across the United States. We started our unit about the 1840s with a few relevant sources. We dissected journal entries and newspaper articles from the era. Then we used an online map program to pinpoint some of the key forts, rivers, and sites along the path.

What followed was the purple cow: game play with the classic Oregon Trail computer simulation on the Free Streaming Internet Archive from Minnesota Educational Computing Consortium (MECC). Until we played the game in class, I never would have thought avoiding death by dysentery could be so enjoyable. Students would take five-minute breaks from game play to journal about their journey through the game.

Game play isn't just about playing around. It's a painless way to learn. There are games and apps for every major subject in school. Search your topic online and in app stores to see what comes up. You might be able to find a virtual experience.

MUSIC—WHAT SONG LYRICS CONNECT WITH THIS LESSON?

My fifth-grade students were having a lot of trouble memorizing the Bill of Rights. While trying to come up with a teaching plan in my living room one night, I heard Will Schuster—the choir teacher from the TV show *Glee*—in the background. I glanced up to see him performing the running man and singing "Ice Ice Baby" to his students.

Wait a minute, I thought, *"Ice Ice Baby" sounds a lot like "Rights Rights Baby."* I spent the next hour turning Vanilla Ice's hit song into a civics lesson rap. We performed it the next day and later made a music video that went viral on YouTube.

We ended up filming the music video on a teacher workday, because I didn't want to cut into more instructional time during school. So thirty kids volunteered to come in and make the video—on their day off! That sent a powerful message to me as a teacher that kids will do anything to be a part of the learning process if I bring purple cows into the classroom.

Pick a song and have your students work in groups of three to four to come up with a few stanzas of their own songs. When they're ready, they can perform their creations in front of the class. It's easier for our brain to remember information presented through rhyme and meter. Use that to your advantage to make the curriculum stick.

> You can check out our "Rights Rights Baby" video on my website justinfashley.com. You can also find materials there to help you write your own songs; download my Song Lyric Remix Creator (or copy it from pages 139–140).

TECHNOLOGY—HOW CAN STUDENTS USE A DIGITAL RESOURCE TO DEMONSTRATE THEIR LEARNING?

After reading about the colonies' grievances against England in the Declaration of Independence, students worked in pairs to imagine how the colonists might complain to King George using today's technology and language. Rather than write them out, they used iphonetextgenerator.com to text the complaints. The acronyms and emoticons the students used took words written in 1776 and brought them to life in our time. I did have to inform one student that "WTF, King George?" wasn't the best choice of letters. Not just because of the implied language, but also because of the lack of detail. "Why 'WTF'? Be specific."

A science teacher on my team at school has her kids create animated comics with PowToon to explain topics such as evolution or the principle of natural selection. There are endless possibilities for using technology to stimulate interest in just about any subject matter. Try tapping into digital tools. This allows students to experience learning in a fun, fresh way.

QUESTIONING—HOW CAN I SUMMARIZE THE ENTIRE LESSON WITH A SINGLE QUESTION?

After an enlightening, eight-hour day of Performance Excellence for All Kids (PEAK) training a few years back, one point from the presenter stood out the most for me: Instead of testing students with a list of questions throughout class, why not have them explore one higher-level thinking question for the whole period? Let kids research the evidence and share their own opinions on a controversial topic in class. Debates, though heated at times, fully engage those who are speaking and listening.

We were studying the Boston Massacre and Tea Party Rebellion around the same time the protests in Ferguson, Missouri, were taking place. I asked students for their take: Are people who protest against their government good or bad citizens of their country? Why? They spent the entire class reading, writing, and arguing with one another. It was awesome. After the bell rang, they kept going. They wanted to finish the debate, even if it meant being tardy for the next class.

Answering highly emotional questions can also intrigue kids. A language arts teacher at my school has her students read about the conditions of concentration camps and listen to testimonies of Holocaust survivors. Then they use their findings in a class discussion about this overarching question: How can a single person create universal change?

Students see multiple choice and true/false questions almost daily. Is it possible to zoom in on one key idea for the lesson you're planning? Something deep, puzzling, or debatable?

SETTING—HOW CAN I USE THE ENVIRONMENT TO ALTER MY STUDENTS' EXPERIENCE?

To teach about the law-making process in the United States, I split the room in two with a line of duct tape across the floor. I moved half the desks to each side. The students on the left were members of the House of Representatives. Those seated on the right were in the Senate. I sat at my desk as the president. The class met in chambers to discuss bills that, if passed, would become new class rules. When a bill passed Congress, a student from the Senate would run it back to me for review, where I could veto it or sign it into law. I vetoed the No Homework Bill, but I did quickly sign the No Nose Picking or Booger Flinging Bill into law.

A math teacher on my team at school turned off the lights after handing his students laser pointers and mirrors. Then he let them use the mirrors to reflect the lasers on various points of the room so they could visualize different angles they were learning about in class.

You can use a setting outside your room, too. While researching the Cold War, my students worked in groups to draw artwork from the Berlin Wall on a wall of the school using sidewalk chalk. They added facts about the Cold War— dates, vocabulary, and various themes to demonstrate what they had learned. Their work conveyed the artistic outcry of the time. They also included key phrases and statistics to teach fascinating facts they uncovered in their research. One group, for example, drew a watchtower with the number 302 inside it. That's how many towers were built along the wall to keep people in East Berlin. Another created a giant hot air balloon; this was one way two families escaped successfully to the West.

Can you restructure the desks or alter the lighting in the classroom? Can you decorate the walls with a theme that matches the learning objective? This is one strategy that keeps students guessing, because they sense the environment every time they walk into the room.

COMPETITION—HOW CAN I USE A COMPETITIVE GAME AS A MOTIVATION TO LEARN?

When examining the Scots-Irish culture, we had our own Highland Games on the playground. After marching out to "Scotland the Brave" that was blaring from my '80s boom box, students ran to their teams. Then they competed in games like the real Scots-Irish people play at festivals each year.

The caber toss challenge requires competitors to throw a tree log as far as they can. The kids threw pool noodles instead of the traditional cabers. In another competition called the sheaf toss, the Scots-Irish use a pitchfork to try to launch a bale of hay over a high pole. We used a broom, a volleyball, and the monkey bars with the same goal in mind.

Think up a contest outside the school or in the classroom to push your content. Or you could use an online game such as Kahoot, where students compete to answer questions on a specific topic covered in class. Each question pops up (one at a time) with four answer choices represented by a specific shape and color. Students use their phones, tablets, or computers to pick the answer they think is correct. The faster they answer, the more points they get, and the top five scorers are posted after each question.

Including a Purple Cow in your lessons isn't just about your students' experience. It's also about your own. I teach six classes of kids each school day. That means if I accidentally plan a boring lesson, I don't just have to live through it once. I have to relive it five more times! You too will spend a large chunk of your time in the classroom on instruction, so make it fun for your kids, as well as you. Go purple!

You can download Purple Cow Clip Art under the Free Stuff tab at my website, justinfashley.com.

Chapter 13

FOCUS

You've probably set goals before, whether they were professional or personal. Maybe at the beginning of a school year your district required you to document a goal that's specific, measurable, attainable, realistic, and timely (SMART) on your professional growth plan. Or maybe you tried making a New Year's resolution in January to shed a few pounds, eat healthier, or save money.

Even if we make a long, bulleted list of everything that needs to be done, choosing where to start can be overwhelming.

If you're like me, you've found the act of goal setting much easier than the execution. Anyone can create goals, but achieving them is another story. A study by the University of Scranton found that a whopping 92 percent of participants failed to achieve their New Year's resolutions. Whether it's a goal related to work or personal life, there are many factors that prevent success. In my opinion, two are very significant:

1. We Get Bored with Our Goals

We live in a culture of instant gratification: one-day shipping, news articles at the click of a button, an entire season of our favorite TV show streaming without commercial interruption. This way of life presents a challenge for goals that can take a year or longer to reach. SMART goals require a lengthy delay of gratification. It's a stretch. When life moves at the speed of desire, it's only natural for us not to want to wait for anything that can't come in an instant.

2. We Get Overwhelmed by Our Goals

Ambitious goals often require multiple tasks over an extended span of time. Even if we make a long, bulleted list of everything that needs to be done, choosing where to start can be overwhelming. In their book *Made to Stick*, Chip and Dan Heath refer to it as *decision paralysis*. Too many things can prevent us from even starting with one thing.

It's good to dream big, but we need to start small. We don't need to figure out the entire route in the beginning. We just need to visualize an endpoint and a first step that builds momentum. The rest can be figured out along the way.

The best tools for solving the problems of boredom and being overwhelmed with goals are a calendar poster where you can record one thing you did to move toward your goal each day, and a daily planner that keeps you focused in a world of distractions.

The calendar should be a small, reusable poster with a box for each day of the week for thirteen weeks, not a year. Set a goal that is achievable in about three months. Doing so keeps you engaged, because the goal is shorter and succinct. At the top of the calendar, I use a dry-erase marker to record one goal. In the boxes under it, I write one thing that I've done to move toward my objective. I do this each night before bed.

> BestSelf Co has examples of these kinds of tools at bestself.co.

Recently, my goal was to produce a historical hip-hop music video called *Straight Intta Oregon* about pioneers who journeyed West in search of a better life. First, I spent several days reading about the Oregon Trail and writing song lyrics. Then I recorded a few stanzas of the song using GarageBand. My calendar helped me envision my plan and keep track of my progress.

I also use a journal each morning to structure my day and stay motivated. I record my target tasks, my successes, and lessons I'm learning. The journal I use even has an inspirational quote on every page. The journal makes the tracking process accessible and uplifting. And I don't feel overwhelmed by the tasks I need to complete to eventually reach my goal, because I'm freestyling it a bit and breaking it all down into manageable steps as I move forward.

There's a sign on the wall in my boxing gym that reads "FOCUS: Follow One Course Until Successful." Whether you use a BestSelf tool or a tool of your own, try shortening the course you're on and do a little something each day to head in the right direction. This can help you FOCUS.

Chapter 14

Stay Organized Throughout the School Year

It's so hard for us to stay organized while school is in session because there is a continual flood of activity. There are so many things coming into and leaving the classroom—paperwork from meetings, IEP plans, lesson materials, and student resources. The following tips can help you keep track of everything, shave hours off your workload, and make you more efficient while at work.

Mark Desk Locations with Duct Tape

At the beginning of each year and whenever you change the desk arrangement, place a piece of colored duct tape at the ends of each row or corners of each table group. After a few hours of students working at their desks and circulating throughout the room, the perfectly aligned arrangement looks as though it's been through an earthquake. At the end of each block or school day, remind students to line up their desks with the tape markers. At the beginning of each block and school day, the first thing the kids see is the furniture. Orderly rows or groupings give a good first impression.

Use a Notebook Task List

If you're like me, you might forget everything you need to do if you don't put it on paper. Once it's on paper, it's trapped! It stays there as a reminder for later, which means you don't have to worry about it each moment of the day. You can release it from your brain and zero in on what matters most right now.

Get a notebook and title the first page Task List. When you are checking your email and remember that you have to send out a newsletter by next week, write it on the Task List. Or when you review next week's mini lesson and realize you need to find one more resource to go with it, write it on the Task List. Everything you need to do that doesn't have a specified time goes on the Task List. Appointments, tasks with a due date, and events with predetermined start times can go on a digital calendar (more on that follows).

For anything that takes a minute or less to accomplish, don't write it on the Task List. Do it as soon as you come across it. If it takes less time to do the task than it does to write it down, just knock it out quickly.

Fit Small Daily Tasks on a Sticky Note

Before you begin each day, place a small sticky note on top of your Task List. This is your daily to-do list. Write the date at the top of the sticky. Then look over your Task List and your calendar. Record each task you're aiming to complete for that day. If all your tasks don't fit on that one sticky, you are cramming too much into one day, my friend! Lower your expectations. Pick only the most critical ones and put the rest back on the Task List.

After you finish each task, cross it off the to-do list for that day and the Task List in your notebook. I get a rush out of crossing through each chore. If you would rather use technology than a notebook and sticky notes, try using an app on your phone or computer to keep up with your tasks.

> Google Now or Siri are great ways to set reminders on your smartphone.

Whether your list is digital or on paper, don't beat yourself up at the end of the day if you don't accomplish everything. Be content with executing about three of every four tasks on the list. In this instance, a 75 percent pass rate is one you can be proud of. In just one day, you put a dent in that big list you've got going.

Go Digital with Schoolwork

When it comes to lesson plans and student work, use technology as often as you can. You can make your paper stack disappear from your desk. Storing it online means you can make it reappear, only when you need it. Your lesson plans can go in Google Drive. Or store them in iCloud. If your class has access to computers or tablets, use Edmodo or a Google Form for instruction and assessments. Let computers do the menial work so you can do everything else.

Place Student Work Bins by the Door

If you use paper for classwork or homework, put paper bins (one for each class or subject) on a table or cart near the door of the room. Label each bin by block number, class period, or subject area. Kids can turn in their work when they come in at the beginning of class or after class ends.

Model for kids how to keep the papers tidy. Show them two bins with paper—one with a neat paper stack and the other a mess with papers sticking out horizontally and vertically. This is a good visual for students. And it sets an explicit expectation. It may seem trivial, but you won't have to flip the papers around and upside down to get them in a neat stack if the kids help you stay organized.

All teachers get hit with distractions. This is annoying and can be discouraging, but it's beatable. Think about implementing new systems. Hone your organizational skills to save time and energy. You'll know where your files are when you need them. You'll have a central list for tasks you need to complete, in the short- and long-term. A day in the life of a teacher can be chaotic, but being organized cuts down on the chaos.

Chapter 15

Find Your Teacher Flow

Two young fish are swimming down a river, and an older fish swims past them in the opposite direction. He says, "Good morning, boys. How's the water?"

They smile at him and swim on. Further up the river, one of the young fish turns to the other and says, "What's water?"

Ken Robinson, an education activist and researcher, shares this story in his book *Finding Your Element* to explain the idea of flow: being so immersed in your environment that you don't even realize you're there. To be clear, everyone's flow is different. Throughout the day, there are various paths you can take that point to the same direction. Your route is determined by you. If you're an introvert, you might not be able to find flow during whole-group discussions. If your parents were divorced, you might find flow in supporting a student who is going through a similar trial.

Flow is specific, not general. Flow is not in everything you do at school. Flow rests in the effortless elements of teaching, in a unit of study that you love to teach or in a club you volunteer to lead.

To make teaching more satisfying, you need to find your flow as often as you can. You can't make flow happen for an entire day, but even a few minutes of flow several times each day is helpful. When you do, it fuels positive emotions and brings about positive results. It gives students and staff members the opportunity to experience your best self. It helps you find meaning in workdays that would otherwise seem mundane.

But how do you know when you've found your teacher flow? And how can you experience more of it each day? Start with metacognition—the act of reflecting on your own thinking in the past and present, so you can pack more meaningful moments into your school day in the future. Here are some ideas to get you started.

A Favorite Teacher

As educators, we all have had teachers in our lives who ignited our desire to teach. It might have been their sense of humor, the way they taught, or the high expectations they had for students. Think about what attracted you to the profession. Do what your favorite teachers did, in your own way of course.

Mrs. McMannie was my ninth-grade writing teacher. She was my favorite. When she saw me quietly crying in the back of her room after my parents split up, she pulled me into the hallway and listened to me as I poured out my heart. She told me that I was strong enough to get through it and that she had a special feeling about me. She felt as though I was going to do something big with my life. And she was right. I became a teacher.

I still have the little inspirational quotes she gave me throughout that semester to encourage me. I speak the same faith to my students when they are discouraged. I start school each August with a giant stack of quote cards on my desk and pass them out throughout the year. The stack of cards dwindles down to a few pieces of paper by June. It brings me so much joy to do for others what she did for me.

A Lost Sense of Time and Place

Think back to lessons, meetings, or downtime at school when you've been totally lost in the moment, when time seemed to stop and nothing else seemed to matter.

When I taught elementary school, I loved facilitating several parts of our Revolutionary War Water Balloon Battle unit. The end goal was to have the students compete in a capture-the-flag game between the British and the Americans. There was so much I enjoyed about that day: seeing the eyes of two students light up when I announced their job as generals, helping them come up with battle plans, discussing real battles and their outcomes, and watching them march out like soldiers. And then there was the moment just after I blew the horn to signal the beginning of the game, when a Patriot launched the first balloon, and it exploded in midair. It all happened in slow motion.

As each year passed, we added a little more fun to the Revolutionary War unit. We had a class debate between Patriots and Loyalists. We added a drummer to each army. And we used tri-fold boards to make hospitals and jails for soldiers who were injured or captured. I know it sounds like a lot of work. But it didn't feel like work. It was flow.

Chapter 16

Make Your Whys Bigger Than Your Why Nots

Why not teach? There are probably thousands of reasons. I can think of twenty-five off the bat:

- short lunch breaks
- migraines
- constantly having to hold your pee
- limited resources
- high-stakes testing
- long work hours
- Vampire Teachers
- 504 plans
- flying boogers
- critical principals
- broken copy machines
- giant stacks of paperwork
- IEP meetings
- long staff meetings
- shrinking school budgets
- large class sizes
- starting salaries

- disrespectful students
- disappearing pension plans
- slow Wi-Fi connections
- puberty
- politicians with all the answers
- boring learning standards
- email overloads
- fart noises

In the book *Teacher Wars*, Dana Goldstein points out that out of all major professions in the United States, teaching is one of the most controversial in the country. Politicians on both sides of the aisle point fingers at failing schools. Media outlets frequently report on student achievement gaps. Conversely, in Finland, teaching is ranked the third most desirable career path in the country. And in South Korea, teachers are regarded as nation builders. In the United States, you know what they say about teachers? "Those who can, do. Those who can't, teach."

In an environment with so much negativity, there are countless reasons why you should not enter or remain in the profession. There are, however, five overpowering reasons why you should make a career out of teaching.

1. Kids

Teachers get to spend their workdays with kids. Because of kids, each day has its own surprises. While many workers stay stuck at a desk or sit through boring meetings, you get to be with children—young people full of joy (maybe in part because they haven't yet been burdened with bills and busyness).

Even though kids can be loud and crazy, they will say silly things that will make you laugh, sweet things that will make you cry, and inspiring things that will move you. You get free entertainment and encouragement from those you serve.

2. Best Teacher Friends (BTFs)

Lasting friendships are born out of a shared struggle. You will work with many teachers, and you'll be lucky enough to make friends with a few of them forever. Even if you change schools, you'll stay in contact. You'll meet up for dinner. You'll reminisce over the good ole days. You'll swap stories like old friends at a high school reunion.

3. Teacher Flow

As we discussed previously in chapter 15, this job gives you the opportunity to find your teacher flow—to escape from work while at work.

When I was rapping the Bill of Rights with my kids, I wasn't working, I was flowing. When I introduced historical figures with our time machine, I wasn't counting the minutes until five. I wasn't at work. I was lost in the moment.

You know exactly what I'm talking about. You've been in the flow. It's priceless. It doesn't happen all day, every day, but it happens enough to remind us why we teach. It's not about the paycheck. It's about the calling. It's about the flow.

> If you're an educator, you need to know that your life is a meaningful one.

4. Community

I'll never forget how discouraging it was to read what a former North Carolina Speaker of the House said about teachers during a state GOP convention in 2011: "Teachers don't care about kids. They don't care about classrooms . . . They only care about their jobs and their pensions."

When the Speaker ran for United States Senator, I volunteered as the education cochair for his opponent, who was also the incumbent at the time. I worked on her campaign team to help other North Carolinians, especially teachers, understand the damage the Speaker had done to our schools when he tried to pass $500-million budget cuts for schools across the state. I volunteered to speak on a TV commercial when he tried to cut the North Carolina Teaching Fellows Scholarship, the scholarship that helped me get my education degree.

On the morning of Election Day, the school where I worked was a polling station. The Speaker showed up about a few yards from my classroom window. He was standing in front of the gym, greeting voters as they entered to cast their ballots. I gazed out at him as my students entered the room behind me. Our eyes met, and then I walked away. *There is no way he is winning this election*, I thought. *We've got him beat.*

Turns out, I was wrong. Later that night while watching TV at home, I watched the results pour in from all over the state. The margin was slim, but he won. It was heartbreaking. I felt so defeated. How in the world could people in my community support a guy who hated teachers? I played around with the idea of taking off the next school day, maybe even looking for another job with more respect. Then I stopped myself. *I will not let this guy stop me from teaching*, I thought. *I will not give him that power.*

I showed up early to school the next day and taught my heart out. I was writing all over the white board, making circles around the room, helping every kid with a smile on my face and a spring in my step. Throughout the day, there were other teachers who popped their heads in my room and even sat with me in the teachers' lounge. They were frustrated about the election results, too, but they didn't let it stop them from teaching. We listened to one another and encouraged one another to continue the course for our kids.

At the end of the school day, I felt as though we had won a fight, even though we lost the election. We showed up. We taught. We beat him by proving him wrong. That's the only way we can win against powerful entities that oppose us. Through community and camaraderie, we can overcome. The path isn't always an easy one, but at least we are in it together.

5. Legacy

Have you ever thought about how you'll die? Or even when? It's morbid, I know, but roll with me for a minute. At most funerals, your entire life story will be condensed into a few minutes. Someone will summarize you in a few paragraphs. People will talk about your family, your upbringing, your career, and your influence on those around you.

If you're buried, a tombstone will be placed on your grave. It will contain two dates: the day you were born and the day you died. You had no say in that first date, and your impact on the second date is questionable, but you completely decide what's in the middle: the dash. The dash, the mark of everything that happened between your birth and death, is your legacy: it's what you did with your life.

Make that dash count. Be a teacher.

My high school music teacher, Mrs. Osmond, died recently. Her funeral gave me goose bumps. Hundreds of people attended. By the time I got there, it was standing room only. The minister said a lot of nice words about her during the ceremony, but I didn't have to hear one word from him to understand how valuable her life really was. All I had to do was look around at all the students, from teenagers to adults now grown, crying for her loss and celebrating her life. It was beautiful.

What will students say about you one day? If you're an educator, you need to know that your life is a meaningful one. The students you teach now will grow up to be stronger, smarter, and happier because of you. Your funeral will be full. Your love will be indelible. Your impact will be incalculable. Your dash will count.

The One Secret All Teachers Who Last Learn Early

Most teachers operate in roughly the same reality. Broadly speaking, they get paid the same when they start out. They have the same class sizes, have the same kinds of students, work at the same schools, and teach with the same curriculum.

Even though our experiences are similar, one teacher's perception of our reality can be different from another's. You have to choose the right perspective about teaching. That perspective is something that teachers who retire after thirty years discover early on in their careers. It's what teachers who quit after a few years never figure out.

It's a mindset. I call it a word cloud mindset.

There are websites you can use to create a word cloud, an artistic combination of any words you type in. They look like this:

The coolest part about word clouds is that you can make some of the words stand out above the others. How? By entering certain words more frequently than others. For example, if you put *kids* in ten times, that overshadows *limited resources* in the word cloud. Or if you copy *legacy* into your word cloud fifteen times, that term suddenly grows far greater than *long work hours.* The word cloud would transform into this:

What we think and talk about has to be the five reasons to teach, not the twenty-five reasons not to. The twenty-five will never disappear, but they can dissipate.

How to Make Your Whys Bigger

Focus on your vocabulary. Your language. Your words. The ones you use when talking to others, and to yourself.

Here's a practical strategy that I've found helpful from *The No Complaining Rule* by Jon Gordon: Anytime you speak a negative sentence, replace the period with a comma and conjunction. Specifically, a *but* or maybe an *or*.

"I don't get paid enough money to teach, *but* at least I get to work a job I love."

"It's taking forever to type up this lesson and get these materials together, *but* my students are going to have so much fun and learn a lot from this lesson when I teach it tomorrow."

Negativity may be all around you, but don't let it get *in* you. I'm not suggesting ignoring the negativity. Just don't give in to it. Make shifting to positives a habit in your conversations and self-talk:

- Another lesson plan to type . . . *or* a chance to get kids excited about your content?

- A news story about how your district is failing . . . *or* a chance to thwart naysayers by showing up every day and teaching your heart out?

- A large class size . . . *or* an opportunity to change even more lives than you anticipated?

These politicians, these budgets, these critics, these parents—all these why nots can't stop you. You're untouchable. These distractors can't destroy your desire to teach. They can't kill you. You were born for this. Teaching isn't just what you do; it's who you are. Use your whys as a constant reminder.

Part Three

PHYSICAL/ EMOTIONAL HAPPINESS

Physical/Emotional Happiness may be the most commonly neglected component of happiness. Your physical and emotional well-being is about your habits involving eating, exercising, and even sleeping.

In this area of life, we have to up our game. If we don't manage our health, we won't have the stamina to win in the other three areas (social, career, and financial). We won't be able to sustain. Sure, we may not feel an immediate impact from going to bed late at night and skipping workouts in the afternoon. But eventually the lack of personal care catches up with us. If you want to enjoy the whole journey of teaching and find that all-important sense of balance, you've got to build the strength to last.

Chapter 17

Survive the Zombie Teacher Apocalypse

Vampire Teachers aren't the only monsters in your school building. There are also Zombie Teachers. Have you seen them before? I saw one just last week. He looked dead, yet he was breathing and alive. He shambled down the hallway as if each step were pulling him closer to the floor. I jumped in the nearest room and shut the door as he got closer. I peeked through the window and shook my head in disbelief as he stumbled by. *He was such a great algebra teacher.* I thought. *I can't believe he's become a zombie.*

Teachers turn into Zombie Teachers, not because of a bite, but because of sleep. Or rather, the lack of it. Even with a double espresso in hand, they zone out in staff meetings. They close their eyes briefly, wishing to get back what they gave up when they became part of the Zombie Teacher apocalypse: a good night's sleep.

For them, there were too many emails to answer, too many students to differentiate for, and too many essays to grade. There wasn't enough time in the workday to get it all done, so they stayed up late at night, losing valuable and much-needed sleep. Whatever it takes, right? Wrong. Your body doesn't care about your intentions, only your actions.

Whatever it takes, right? Wrong. Your body doesn't care about your intentions, only your actions.

There is rarely enough time in the school day to check off everything on the to-do list. But if you choose to stay up late and complete the work at home, think about the possible effects:

- You lose energy the next day, not just for a few hours, but for the entire day.

- You are grumpier, less patient, and more negative around students and teachers.

- You weaken your immune system while working in a room jammed full of germs.

- You upset the cycle of sleep your body expects for nights that follow.

The fastest way to burnout on the job is to become a Zombie Teacher, to choose work over sleep. We tell our students to get plenty of rest the night before a big test, but often we don't practice what we preach.

We must take our own advice every night because we need to teach the next day—and teaching is its own test. Being well rested improves your performance, increases your long-term memory, and lifts your mood. This will allow you to accomplish more in the time you have.

Are you already a Zombie Teacher? Or are you becoming one? If so, your future isn't hopeless. Zombies are zombies forever, but Zombie Teachers can become normal, healthy teachers again.

If you are sleep-deprived, it's likely that you need to sleep *longer* and *better*—more efficiently. It's not always that easy. It might take tossing and turning for an hour or so just to get comfortable and fall asleep. Or maybe you've started waking up a few times each night. Whatever the symptom, you can achieve longer and better sleep by altering three factors: your environment, exercise, and eating habits. I like to call them the three Es for more zzzz's.

Environment

According to *Eat, Move, Sleep* by Tom Rather, it may help to drop the temperature at home two to four degrees each night before you get in bed or trade heavier blankets for lighter ones. A slight drop in body temperature actually induces sleep. Being a little colder in bed will help you fall asleep faster and sleep sounder than you would at your regular room temperature.

When you lay down for bed, try not to use your phone, especially for work-related tasks, such as checking your email. Scrolling through your inbox may not seem like a big deal, but what if you read a spiteful message from a parent that gets you fired up? Or what if your principal asks you to turn in something by the end of the week? Then what happens?

Those emails will keep you awake long after your phone goes to sleep. When in bed, try not to use your phone until the next morning. If you can't resist the temptation, delete your work email from your phone and check it at work. It's hard at first, but it works.

> Whatever the symptom, you can achieve longer and better sleep by altering three factors: your environment, exercise, and eating habits. I like to call them the three Es for more zzzz's.

Exercise

Exercise during the day can help you sleep better at night. But for me personally, there are days where I don't have time to work out, like on curriculum night or when we have a class field trip. Sometimes I'm too busy, and, to be honest, sometimes I'm just too tired.

What I've noticed, though, is that there is typically a trade-off: If I can exercise for just thirty minutes during the day, I will fall asleep almost immediately after getting in bed, and I will sleep really well throughout the night. But if I don't exercise, I end up tossing and turning for up to an hour at night, and I don't feel as well rested when I wake up the next morning.

So on days where my schedule is packed or I'm coasting on fumes, this is what kicks me into gear. I tell myself, *If I can exercise for just thirty minutes today, I will sleep longer and better the whole night.* It doesn't have to be an intense workout. Maybe you can turn on a favorite playlist and do push-ups and sit-ups in your living room when you get home from school. Or you could try jogging around your neighborhood after dinner. Either way, you're moving. And movement is what matters, because it can help you stay still and asleep when you are in bed.

Eating Habits

While breakfast and lunch directly impact your day, your dinner (and snacks or drinks) greatly influences your night. Before going to bed, avoid eating sugary foods or drinking anything that contains caffeine, such as coffee, tea, or sodas. Instead, stick with water or a decaffeinated drink so you can fall asleep faster.

I recently tried out a new app called Sleep Cycle. It logs your personal sleep characteristics over time. Each night before bed, I activated the app and briefly answered a few questions: whether I ate sugary foods before bed, what I had to drink after dinner, and the level of exercise I had completed during the day. Then I placed the phone on the edge of my bed. Throughout the night, Sleep Cycle sensed my movements and determined which phase I was in: awake, light sleep, or deep sleep. When I tossed and turned a lot, I was awake. When I moved around a little, I was sleeping lightly. When I was completely still, I was getting genuine deep sleep.

After gathering the data for a few weeks, I pulled up the sleep chart (in the form of a line graph) from the app and noticed two trends. The first was obvious. It took longer to fall asleep on nights when I had sugary foods or caffeine during or after dinner. My body couldn't settle down until eleven or twelve at night. I expected this. But the second trend is what shocked me: The caffeine and sugar didn't just delay my sleep for a few hours; it disrupted my sleep for the entire night. At around two, three, and four o'clock in the morning, I began moving restlessly and continued to do so for several minutes before falling back into a brief sleep.

Partly because of what I ate and drank before bed, I had destroyed my rhythm. There were spikes all over the graph, instead of a somewhat straight, vertical line. If you can keep caffeine and sugar out of your body at night, you can help your body power down.

A day of teaching is tiring enough, even when you're fully rested, but going into school already tired will result in a whole other level of exhaustion by the day's end.

Chapter 18

Ditch the Teacher Desk

There was a valid reason my teeth were grinding in agony. Namely, my teacher desk. I'm still uncertain as to which was worse: the pain of pulling it out the classroom door or the headache I got from the maddening screech it made as I did so.

It was just a day before open house, and I had made the last-minute decision to ditch my desk. I gladly confess this loony idea was not my own. Mr. Plyler, a BTF, shared it with me. I decided to give it a try, but not before inquiring, "Why did you do this?"

His end goal, he revealed, was twofold: to improve his health and his teaching. His first point made sense. He could easily burn more calories by standing and moving more each school day. But I was puzzled by his second claim. How would his students benefit from the desk removal? Proximity, he explained. Without a corner of his own to escape to, his only option was to move toward his students. There was no place for him to retreat. He could better support small groups because he was always closer. He could more easily monitor off-task behavior, because he was constantly circling the room. There was no longer a physical, or psychological, barrier between him and his kids. I don't know if it was his reasoning or genuine enthusiasm for the idea he was selling, but I bought it. Hence, the teeth grinding. But it wasn't long before I understood the wisdom of his words.

> We sit, sometimes for hours at a time, doing our job at school or home. But the human body is built for movement.

The Benefits of Ditching the Desk

My friend had been right. I saw noticeable improvements within weeks. My daily step count had tripled since I'd left the desk behind. I also felt closer to my kids. I was more aware of those who needed help. And students were voluntarily asking more questions. They were more open to shooting their hands up when I was walking nearby than when I was seated on one end of the room.

It was as though I'd built a treadmill for me and a bridge for my kids. When I'm not teaching in the front of the room, I'm making my way around it. I eventually learned that I couldn't stand all day. Sometimes my knees ache a little, and I need a seat. When I need to sit, I sit at an empty student desk.

There's a third bonus that my friend never mentioned: room space. I currently teach middle school, and I've got thirty-three teenagers in each class. Some of these teens are bigger than me. My desk made the room more cramped than it had to be. Without it, there was now a spot for an extra learning station and more space for brain break games.

As noted in *Get Up* by James Levine, workers over the last few decades have begun to sit more often than ever before. Computers, tablets, and smartphones are now commonplace for work. As teachers, we take attendance, read incoming emails, record grades, and create lesson plans while sitting down with a device. We sit, sometimes for hours at a time, doing our job at school or home. But the human body is built for movement. Granted, we need to sit, rest, and recharge in small doses, but our anatomy is functioning properly when we are upright and active for most of the day.

I'm not going to lie here. Ditching your desk takes a lot of work. Just getting it out of the room (and reorganizing) is a lengthy, exhausting process. And for the first few weeks without my desk, I honestly felt more tired. But after a while, my body adjusted. The aches and lethargy went away. And I started feeling as though I had more energy and endurance each day, not less, than I did the school year before.

If you think this might be of benefit, you may find that ditching your desk is worth it. The outcome, for me at least, made the struggle worthwhile. If you're all in, here's how you can make the adjustment after you move your desk to a supply room:

HOW TO GET BY WITHOUT A DESK

- **Complete paperwork at a student desk or in the media center.** During planning, before school, or after school, find an alternative spot to spread out and knock out grades, email messages, and lesson plans.

- **Store supplies on the side.** Move the basic utensils (paper clips, rubber bands, pens, etc.) to a drawer or cabinet on the side of the room. This gives you quick access when you need the supplies, whether you are in the middle, front, or back of the classroom.

- **Put your computer, projector, and printer on a rolling cart.** If you can't find an empty rolling cart in the school supply room or media center, you can use your teacher ID to get a discount on one at most office supply stores. Make sure to use an extension cord for power. By doing this, you can take the projector anywhere when you want to display a photo or video for the class.

This is a ton of work, I know. But the good news is you only have to do it one time. You are setting up a new system, and once it's operative, you can enjoy the benefits indefinitely.

IF YOU DON'T WANT TO DITCH IT

You may not be a fan of this idea. Maybe you don't want to say good-bye to your desk, or maybe, because of a physical limitation or disability, you can't. I get it. So let's brainstorm an alternative: Is there a way you can be more mobile during the school day? Can you get away from your desk without getting rid of it?

In *The Well-Balanced Teacher*, Mike Anderson shares some great ideas to help teachers strengthen their step game, such as walking to students' desks when they have a question, rather than calling them over to the teacher desk. When small groups rotate through workstations, Anderson suggests making it a goal to walk to each station—once, twice, maybe even three times—as you monitor students and answer their questions.

I even park my car in the last row of the school parking lot so I have to walk farther to get to my room. This adds maybe fifty steps when I enter and exit each day. That's not much, but when you add that up with a lot of other little daily shifts and multiply it by 180 days of school, that's a large number. Look for ways to stay active at school.

There really are two viable options we have here: to do one big thing (ditch the desk), or do several small things (walk to student desks and circulate around the room). Either option can lead us to the same place. Both routes can lead to a happier, healthier teacher.

Chapter 19

Reclaim Your Recess

When you were a kid in school, you were given time to play each day. You probably counted down the minutes until you could break free from your seat and hit the playground. What did you do at recess? Maybe you played tag with a few friends, kicked a soccer ball around, or flew down the slide and climbed the monkey bars.

Now for a few tougher questions: What were your teachers doing while you were at play? Did they play, too? Or did they monitor you while you were living it up? Did they join in the games you played, or did they sit and watch from a distance?

When I first started teaching, I did what I saw my teachers do when I was a kid: I sat and watched my class enjoy their recess. It's a job, after all. I don't remember exactly when it happened, but one day I got tired of sitting and watching kids have fun, so I decided to join them. My principal was cool with the idea of me being a teacher/part-kid at recess.

I would change into a pair of tennis shoes before I lined up my class to walk outside. Then I would play whatever game I wanted to play. If I felt like playing football, I would run all-time quarterback. If I was in the mood for basketball, I would play with the smaller of the two teams at play. While I played, I was also the referee. Without me in the game, kids would argue about pass interferences and foul calls. When I was in the game, they didn't fight. My calls were final. I got my exercise, they played together, and we all had fun.

Some states require students to have at least thirty minutes of scheduled exercise each school day, but teachers deserve it, too. No one tells us we can't play. We've just been conditioned to think we shouldn't. Our own predisposition limits our thinking.

Have you thought about challenging the norm? Maybe you teach at a middle school or high school where games aren't played at recess. Our eighth graders participate in half an hour of teen time, where they talk and walk around the school track. A few teachers sit on the bleachers or stand by the track-and-field fence. They go back and forth between checking their watches and watching students walk. That's too boring for me. I walk and talk with the kids.

If you work at a school where there is no allotted recess time, try to find student-free slots in your schedule, such as lunch, planning periods, before school, or right after. Can you squeeze in ten minutes of walking the track at the beginning of your planning? You could even partner up with another teacher to share lesson and class management ideas while you walk. Or whenever you have a grade-level or team meeting, you could take a longer route to get there. Instead of walking down the hallway, take a scenic route outside, around the school or on a sidewalk between buildings. If part of your teaching duties is outside the school, you have an advantage that many workers who are stuck in the office all day miss out on: you can break free and move while you work.

If the opportunity is there, tap into student recess time to exercise. It's a stress-releaser. You can't add time to your day, but you might be able to reinvent what you do with it.

Chapter 20

Remove School Reminders at Home

Thoughts about teaching flood in and out of a teacher's brain thousands of times each day. We often think about school, even when we're not there, because we are surrounded by quiet, subtle reminders that mentally take us back to the workplace. The stimulus could come in the form of a sight, smell, sound, or conversation. And it's more powerful than we might think.

The Power of a Trigger

In *Contagious*, Jonah Berger explains that sounds and objects, such as signs and pictures, can serve as triggers to memories in our past. Triggers aren't necessarily violent. They're more like a cause-and-effect scenario that takes place in your brain.

For example, let's say you are walking down an aisle at the store. You notice the posters and markers in the office supplies section. That sight takes you back to the poster project your students completed last quarter. Why is that? The poster at the store triggered you to think about posters at school.

Triggers can easily influence thoughts, but they can also impact actions, even at the ballot box. In one study during the 2000 Arizona general election, Berger explains how voter trends were affected by polling locations. Specifically, constituents were voting on a school-bond referendum. If passed, the 0.6 percent sales tax hike would raise money for public schools in the area. Of the citizens who cast their vote, 40 percent voted in churches, 26 percent voted in schools, and 10 percent voted in community centers. And even though the referendum was fiercely debated by both sides, the measure passed.

The oddest thing about it was, of those who cast their ballots in a school, voters chose to support the tax increase by a measure of more than ten thousand. The support was far higher at schools than it was at community centers or churches. Voters who walked through hallways filled with students and smelly lockers were far more likely to vote yes than no. This data suggests two lessons for us: hidden triggers have the power to influence the way we think, and we might want to consider having every school in our country be a polling location when we vote on supporting schools.

But seriously, these reminders, whether they evoke positive or negative memories, can steal you away from the present moment. While it's not possible to fully eliminate these school triggers, you can minimize your exposure to many of them, especially at home. You may find it helpful to start by removing or limiting these five common reminders from your house or apartment:

1. school-related email messages

2. school-related paperwork

3. school-related to-do lists

4. school-related attire

5. school-related conversations

In some cases, you can do more than get rid of these school reminders; you can also replace them with positive triggers that reinforce your home life. Let's start with school communication.

> Remember, if it's out of sight, it's out of mind. Don't feel guilty about removing these reminders from your home. You are not turning your back on teaching.

School-Related Email Messages

Try not to check your work email on your phone or on your laptop at home. You can answer email when you get to school each morning, for a few minutes during planning, and right before you leave in the afternoon. You don't check for mail from the post office twenty times a day, and you don't need to do so with your school email either.

School-Related Paperwork

The stack of unit tests that sit on your counter all weekend long loom over you until they are graded Sunday night before bed. Every time you walk near the papers, you remember that work awaits you. If you have to bring schoolwork home, keep it out of sight. Store it in the back floorboard of your car, in your trunk, or in a closet. Don't take it out until you're ready to knock it out. Or free up your schedule so it doesn't leave the classroom. And maybe put the free counter space to use—display your weekend plan or family field trip list (see chapters 7 and 8). This helps you stay present during the weekend and look forward to ones in the future.

School-Related To-Do Lists

If you are like me and can't function without a to-do list, try keeping two separate lists instead of one. Store a list for school tasks in your classroom and keep one at home for things outside of school.

It's okay if a task such as shopping for class supplies spills over to your to-do list for the weekend because you couldn't get it done after school during the workweek. Some things will naturally intermix, but most tasks should be sorted into the right place. Have one list for school and another for household chores. Start a Google Doc if you absolutely have to add things to the list while you are at home. If your preference is paper, store the school list at school. Keep your home list in the kitchen or on a desk at home.

School-Related Attire

Bring your dress clothes out only when you need them, like on school spirit day or when you have to get snazzed up for an observation. Dress clothes or T-shirts with the school logo should be hung up in the back corner of your closet or on the backside of your closet door. You can also hide them, neatly folded at the bottom of a drawer so they don't poke out over the items above them. As I mentioned in a previous chapter, one of my students died in a car accident. He loved tie-dye, and we had a tie-dye day at school to honor him. Whenever I see the hippy-ish blue and purple shirt I wore that day, I think about his tragic death. I keep the shirt in the bottom drawer. I know exactly where it is if I need it, but I don't expose myself to it every morning when I'm getting dressed.

School-Related Conversations

Protect your ears against conversations in group settings with family at the dinner table or neighbors in the front yard. The topic of teaching might come up. Some people love talking about education. Most times I do, too. But make sure any conversations you engage in are building you up and not depleting your energy in some way. If the conversation turns negative or is draining, give short responses and think of something positive to share. Then change the topic to anything else. Do the unthinkable and talk about religion or politics. Anything to avoid hearing the well-meaning, but clichéd reminder that "They don't pay teachers enough money."

Remember, if it's out of sight, it's out of mind. Don't feel guilty about removing these reminders from your home. You are not turning your back on teaching. You are compartmentalizing it: organizing objects, thoughts, and emotions where they belong. You are removing distractions outside school so that when you are at school, you can give it your full attention.

Chapter 21

Make Your Classroom Your Happy Place

Corporations pay ad agencies millions of dollars each year to sum up their companies in a few words or, preferably, a recognizable symbol. Like we discussed in the last chapter about school reminders at home, these images can serve as triggers. But you aren't just surrounded by them at your house. They're also at your school. Some things at school may evoke memories of past mistakes or bad experiences you'd rather forget. All it takes is one subtle reminder, and, before you can stop it, your brain goes to the one place you don't want it to go. While you can't remove all negative reminders at school, you can counter many of them with something more positive.

> By manipulating your environment, you are outsmarting your brain.

Update Your Wallpapers, Screensavers, and Backgrounds

What type of wallpaper do you have on your computer? Is it a blank screen? Is it a factory pic of a mountain or a beach? Is it a meaningful family picture?

Instead of seeing random images before you log in, treat yourself to adventures from your past that mean something. Search through your digital photo albums to find photos of your favorite memories. Then fuse them into technology you use at work, so you can crack a smile every time you open the device:

- **Showcase favorite people on your phone and tablet background and wallpaper.** Display pictures of your favorite shared experiences, such as the time you took a special vacation with your best friend, when you kissed your spouse in your wedding ceremony, or while you were surrounded by close friends and family at your bat mitzvah.

- **Showcase favorite accomplishments on your computer background.** Display pictures that remind you of past successes, such as a cap and gown photo from college graduation or photos from an awards ceremony.

Get a Throwback Desktop Calendar

The bulky calendar that used to be on our work desks is now considered obsolete in most schools. Today, we often stay organized by placing IEP meeting times and assignment due dates on digital calendars. A computer calendar beats out a paper copy in almost every way: you can check your daily schedule on your phone before you leave home or you can share the date a guest speaker is visiting your grade with other teachers on your team.

Teachers typically need to use digital calendars to keep track of school related events, but what about recreational tasks outside of school? If you are still using a desk, put it to good use with a colorful desk calendar. Record only recreational tasks on it. It's for fun stuff only. With a colorful sharpie, write out your softball team schedule for the season or label your upcoming family field trips to the mountains and the beach. Pencil in the upcoming dinner date with your best friend.

If you no longer have a desk because you ditched it (per my advice in chapter 18), hang the calendar above a filing cabinet or on a bulletin board in the back of the room. Next time you fill out a 504 form or retrieve a file from a cabinet drawer, you might glance at the calendar reminder and note that more enjoyable experiences are on the way.

Post Your Weekend Plan in Your Weekly Work Station

Each Monday, sketch out a loose plan for the weekend, like the one in the Follow a Weekend Plan chapter. Then position it in a place where you'll see it often. I post mine on the right side of my teacher cart, near my daily to-do list. I can easily see it and quickly add to it as I go from Monday to Friday.

Decorate Student Desks with Laminated Curriculum

Students desks are also unclaimed territory. Think about a curriculum tool that could be laminated and taped to their desks. Every desk in our room has a U.S. map on top of it and a sock with a dry erase marker inside it. Whenever we're studying about Americans migrating to California or the South and North dividing in the Civil War, kids take out their markers and map out the events in front of them. When they're done, they wipe off their writing with the sock.

The desk decoration gives the students a visual connection to content we're learning about, but it also benefits me. It provides a fun, colorful pop to the otherwise plain desks whenever I walk into the room and see them or sit down at one to do work.

Have Students Make Positive Posters

At the beginning of the school year, let your kids in on the fun. For classwork or homework, have them research online for a quote on happiness. When they find one they love, get them to write the quotation and author name, and draw a colorful picture that symbolizes the phrase. They could create it on a poster board or construction paper.

If you make their posters a part of your room decor, you can improve the well-being of everyone in the room.

In *Happy for No Reason*, Marci Shimoff and Carol Kline cite research showing that people have about 60,000 thoughts each day. About 48,000 of those are negative. It's possible that several bad thoughts are inspired by objects in our own

> Recitethis.com is a great, free website that lets students create posters with creative backgrounds.

classrooms. We can cut this number significantly through implanting positive triggers. Do this at the beginning of each school year and periodically throughout it. By manipulating your environment, you are outsmarting your brain. With just a little attention to your classroom right now, you can redirect thousands and thousands of thoughts in the days to come.

Part Four

FINANCIAL HAPPINESS

Financial Happiness is financial freedom that can mean worrying less about being able to pay your bills on time each month. Or not having to worry about getting another job after you retire from teaching. But even deeper, financial happiness is a positive mindset about money—that even though we don't make millions, we can make enough to be secure and happy.

With financial freedom, it's easier to focus on what matters most to you. Maybe that means you can focus on buying healthier foods at the grocery store, even if they cost a little more. Or maybe you can pay for professional development sessions when your school or district won't cover the expense. It might mean you've got a bigger budget for family field trips or shopping outings with friends. Your success with money can increase your stock value in every other part of your life.

All we need is a strategy and a few skill sets—for spending, saving, and investing—that we can easily put to work with each paycheck. Bringing balance to your financial side will ripple out and have positive repercussions for your health, career, and relationships.

Chapter 22

Get to Your Gold

Teachers don't teach for the paycheck is a popular phrase you've likely heard or even used before. We know going into the profession that the pay isn't always good. It's not like we're trying to get rich. But why do we believe that being a teacher disqualifies us from being wealthy?

One reason is comparison. When we look around at neighbors, family, and friends who have jobs as important as ours, we notice a gap between the way they live and how we live. Their house is a lot newer. Their car is a lot nicer. Their paycheck *must* be bigger.

There's some truth to this notion. In *Teachers Have It Easy,* Daniel Moulthrop, Nínive Clements Calegari, and Dave Eggers note that out of all major professions requiring a four-year college degree, public school teachers earn some of the lowest starting salaries and receive some of the slowest pay increases as they grow in experience. Some of the students we teach will have larger paychecks than us, just a few years after they graduate from college.

A second reason we feel we can't be wealthy is lack of opportunities. Aside from a decent salary bump for earning a master's degree or getting nationally board certified, there aren't a lot of options for significantly increasing our teacher pay. Still, many of us scrape by, living paycheck to paycheck, month to month. Even if we are winning in every other arena of life—at work, at home, and in our health—losing with our money can cost us. For a lot of teachers, finances can be frustrating. We make such a small amount, and yet there is so much to pay for—college loans, rent, groceries, and school supplies. The struggle is real.

Teachers Who Want Wealth

Believe it or not, there are teachers who have figured out how to have the best of both worlds—how to teach and still have wealth. They're not millionaires, but they are financially free. They don't worry about money. They've figured out how to master the game.

But before we go any further, let's break down the mindset of a wealthy teacher. What do rich teachers believe about money? What do they think about it? What do they know that most teachers don't? Teachers with wealth can vary in many ways—age, background, gender, teaching subject, or experience level. However, the one thing most have in common is a similar viewpoint about wealth.

TEACHERS WHO WANT WEALTH TEACH THEMSELVES ABOUT MONEY

In *Rich Dad, Poor Dad,* financial coach and author Robert Kiyosaki explains that, as students, most of us didn't learn about money in school. We were taught science, math, social studies, and literacy but not financial literacy.

With this in mind, teachers who want to increase their wealth educate themselves about spending, saving, and investing. They listen to audiobooks and podcasts, read blog posts, take online courses, network with professionals outside of the field, and ask advice from financially literate friends and family. Eventually, they decode the meaning of money and begin to understand how the market works.

TEACHERS WHO WANT WEALTH ENVISION WINNING THE GOLD

Michael Phelps, considered by many to be the greatest Olympian of all time, was all about vision. During his training for swimming, Phelps's coach gave him a homework assignment outside of the pool. Every night, just before he went to bed, and every morning, as soon as he woke up, he had to close his eyes and envision himself in slow motion, swimming the perfect race. He's gone on to win twenty-three gold medals in Olympic venues around the globe, but success started with his vision.

Teachers who want wealth also have a vision, for their finances. They have a personal, mental picture of what wealth looks like. To make this vision a reality, they plan. They make a plan for monthly spending, investing, and retirement. They have an investment plan. They set goals, based on numbers and percentages, such as "I will have $10,000 in my savings account by the end of this year" or "I will decrease my eating out experiences by 10 percent this month."

TEACHERS WHO WANT WEALTH ARE WILLING TO SWEAT LONGER AND WORK HARDER

Teachers who have a sense of financial freedom make money outside of the classroom. It's really tough to be wealthy if teaching is the only income you're banking on, so they worked side hustles during the school year or they had summer gigs. Adding to their annual incomes gave them more wiggle room to spend, save, and invest.

If you're entertaining this idea, a word of caution: A second job will require a few nights and weekends or a few workweeks in the summertime. Don't over-book yourself. These extra hours should be done minimally. Remember, you've still got to balance with your school work and free time with family and friends.

TEACHERS WHO WANT WEALTH ARE GRATEFUL FOR BRONZE (BEFORE THEY GET THEIR GOLD)

For teachers, especially rookies, it's easy to fall into a comparison trap. You might compare where you're at with teachers who are more experienced, who have been teaching longer, and therefore might appear to have more than you. This leads to discouragement when there are so many people around you who seem wealthier. You work just as hard as they do, maybe even harder, and yet you can't live like they live. But those kinds of comparisons make it harder to appreciate what you've already achieved.

Mike Cernovich, author of *Gorilla Mindset*, discusses a study that evaluated the facial expressions and postevent interviews of athletes who participated in the 1992 Olympic Games and 1994 Empire State Games. Researchers discovered that medalists who won bronze were happier than those who got the silver. Why? Because of their point-of-view. The silver medalists were milliseconds from a gold medal. If they would have swum a little smoother or sprinted a little harder, they could have won. By comparing their position to someone above them, they were left unsatisfied. While I'm

> We make such a small amount, and yet there is so much to pay for—college loans, rent, groceries, and school supplies. The struggle is real.

sure the bronze medalists wanted to win, too, they had a different perspective. They hadn't yet earned the gold, but they were content with what they had for that moment.

When you are first getting started, a key to getting to the gold faster is to avoid comparisons and be grateful for the bronze. It's not your dream life, but you can cover your basic needs, something many people in the world are unable to do. You still have your vision for gold and that will push you toward it. You'll get there eventually. But until then, you can still be happy with a bronze.

Chapter 23

Act Younger Than Your Wage

Why don't you have a plan for spending and saving? In a moment of introspection, I asked myself this question in 2015 when I was twenty-nine-years old and broke. My bank account balance totaled less than a hundred dollars.

My initial excuse for not having a budget plan was that I didn't know how to make one. And worse, I didn't want to learn. To me, the process was confusing. Where do I start? How much should I try to spend on gas? Clothes? Food?

A second reason for resisting a budget was the limitations. If I make the plan, I have to follow it. This means I have to cut away all my wants. No more books at the bookstore. No more expensive coffee. No more quality clothes.

Still, I knew I couldn't continue my freestyle spending. I couldn't even pay all my bills between paychecks without the help of a credit card. Living month to month with little to no money made me miserable. I knew I needed to take action, so I found and used an online template to quickly create a plan, and then I put the plan to work.

Do You Have a Budget Plan?

Maybe you're like me and in a similar place financially. Or maybe you've got enough cash in the bank, but you feel stagnant, unable to add to your savings or investment. No matter your circumstances, if you don't have a plan for spending and saving, why not? If you want to be financially secure, a budget plan is essential.

A budget keeps track of where every penny is going. It also highlights damaging spending patterns so that we can get rid of them. This means digging out of the barely getting by, month-to-month mindset and looking at the years down the road.

It may seem tedious, but with the right tool in hand, it will take you only a few minutes at the beginning of each month to create a budget plan. Monitoring it and following through gets a little easier with each day. To get started, just choose a format you prefer—either paper or digital.

A Paper Budget Plan

I like using pencils. I enjoy writing things out with a pencil and making corrections with an eraser. And whenever possible, I prefer using paper over a computer because it's tangible and easier on the eyes. So I make a plan on paper each month for my money. You can find several budgets by looking up "monthly budget templates" online.

The template I use is great because it's structured with categories such as utilities, food, and recreation. Even better, there's a suggested percentage amount for each category that serves as a gauge for how much I should allocate. On the first day of each month, I record the amount I expect to spend in each area under the Budgeted column. At the end of the month, I pull up my bank account online and pencil in the actual amount I spent in the Spent column. I try to get the difference between these two numbers to be as close as possible, and I've gotten better at it over time. When I'm done totaling it all up, I use the data in front of me to make minor tweaks to the budget plan for the next month. For example, I spend a little less on to-go food and a little extra on groceries, and put the difference in cost into savings.

> For a free, easy-to-use online budget template, try Dave Ramsey's Cash Flow Plan at daveramsey.com.

A Digital Budget Plan

If you prefer a digital plan over paper, there are some clear benefits. The most notable benefit is convenience. You can access the budget from your computer or phone anywhere. It can also be a time-saver. With paper, you've got to rewrite everything. But with copy and paste, you can quickly keep any part of the budget that doesn't need to be changed.

A good digital budget planner will give you vibrant pie charts, so you can visualize your budget. It makes the process a bit more fun, and it can make your information easier to understand. You can also sign up for email alerts when bills are due, track your investments, and look up your credit score, all through this one tool.

> I once used a digital plan called Mint (mint.com). It's free and comes with a user-friendly smartphone app. It takes a while to set up, but once that's done, using it is easy.

The Subtle Trick to Saving Quicker and Faster

A budget plan can point you in the right direction, but there's a secret strategy that can accelerate you farther, faster. It requires a tiny twist to your monthly plan, with a major payout. I call it acting younger than your wage.

Most teachers receive incremental pay raises each year, or every few years, based on a step scale. The longer you teach, the more experienced you are, the more money you make. Even for states that don't use salary steps, teacher wages slowly trend upward, not down. When you are planning out your budget for each month this school year, pretend you are stuck with the previous year's wages. Find your take-home pay from a year-old pay stub or on your bank account online. Plug that number into your bottom line.

Can you survive on this amount? You made it work last year, so it's possible to do it again. The difference between your past and current annual salary is minimal when broken down by month, so you won't feel a drastic cut, just a trim. People tend to spend a little more when they make more: A bigger TV. A car with lower mileage. A new pair of shoes. It's tempting to indulge, but to live younger than your wage, you can't give in. Your lifestyle should reflect the idea that you have less money than you actually do.

The money you save each month will be a small surplus you can count on. Maybe fifty dollars. Or even a hundred. Whatever the total, consider these suggestions for how to use the extra money:

- **Pay off your debt faster.** Debt requires you to pay back the amount you were lent, plus interest with each monthly payment. Debt creates a downward trend in your financial life. It takes more and more from your bank account each month. But if you can get ahead on payments, you can reverse the trend. The lenders want you to pay the minimum, because it means they make more in interest, but paying off debt ahead of schedule means you pay less.

- **Build your savings to last longer.** Life happens. A hospital visit. A car accident. A house fire. With cash on hand, you can cover those unexpected costs so you don't have to take out loans, get behind on payments, or ruin your credit score.

- **Make investments that will grow bigger.** Small investments, whether in bonds or stocks, have the potential to grow exponentially when they remain untouched over a long span of time. This is called compounding; as your profit grows, you have more money to invest and, in turn, can make more money.

On a side note, some years, due to geography or the economic climate, your cost of living might increase. Don't be alarmed by this. Even if rent goes up, or the price of gas skyrockets to five dollars per gallon, you can work a side hustle during the school year or for a few weeks in the summertime (more on this later). Even with changes in cost of living, this process works. In just three years, I used this method to completely pay off my credit card and substantially improve my retirement plan.

Henry David Thoreau once said that "Almost any man knows how to earn money, but not one in a million knows how to spend it." Before I put my heart into putting together a plan, I was like almost any man or woman. But now, I'm one of the select few Thoreau spoke about; I truly know how to spend the money I make.

Be disciplined about your budget plan. When you put effort into making a thorough lesson plan, accounting for every minute of instruction, you feel a lot better during that lesson than one that you threw together quickly. Writing a budget plan isn't always fun, but the money you save because you wrote the plan will allow you to have more fun. Make sure your needs are covered. Find small ways to cut back. Stream TV for a year instead of paying more for cable or satellite. Buy your clothes at discount retailers rather than pricier clothiers. Cut out the small stuff. For the first few months of planning, you will forget to account for many things, and there will be little emergencies that might pop up: an unexpected hospital bill, a flat tire, a parking ticket. But if you plan ahead, you've got a basic blueprint.

With some of these small adjustments, money could be one less thing in life to stress about, not because you have stacks of dough lying around, but because you know how you are going to spend—and actually save—some of the cash you earn. This frees you up to focus on more important things: teaching, your health, and your relationships.

Chapter 24

Work Every Summer

To teachers, summers are sacred. No schoolwork. No meetings. No agenda. No chatter. With the extra hours and added stresses each school year, we deserve the off-season. It's a time for sleeping in late, shopping with friends, cleaning out the garage, and getting outside for exercise and fresh air. But what about work? A summer job?

"No. Absolutely not."

If this is your thinking, I hear you. I get it. But consider these two benefits of working a part-time job in the summer, even if it's just for three or four weeks.

Money

If you are receiving a paycheck for only ten months out of the year, the two months off can be a stretch financially. After I take the first week off, I work for one month as a summer camp counselor. The extra cash helps pay the bills and fully funds a family vacation to the mountains or beach before school returns. I don't have to tap into my teacher salary to cover it.

Maybe the past school year really burned you out. If you work for a few more weeks, even though you're exhausted, you could spend the bonus on a cruise ticket to get away or on a few home renovations.

Consistency

The transition from the two months of vacation to the first month of school is like going from zero to a hundred miles per hour in a second. It's hard for the brain and body to change so quickly, so a part-time gig maintains the workweek routine and makes for a smoother transition back into the classroom.

Search within Your Network

If you are interested in finding a summer job, start looking for opportunities by asking people you know. Since other teachers are operating on the same schedule, talk to your colleagues to figure out if, when, and where they work during the break. They could help you get your foot in the door and get hired. If not, ask family, friends, and search online for positions.

See Beyond the Salary

If you find a few options, don't choose one or the other solely based on the salary. Look for hidden costs, what expenses come from each position, and what you would have to give up by taking the job.

I'm advising this based on my own personal failure to do this a few summers back. I had planned to work my regular summer counselor job when I was offered a position as a camp director on the other side of town, in downtown Charlotte. It was double the counselor salary, even larger than my monthly teacher pay. I quit the counselor job and started work as a camp director without much thought.

Whether it's inside or outside the home, you can add a little to the piggy bank if you work for just a few weeks each summer.

But there were costs I hadn't foreseen. Because of city traffic, the commute to work took over an hour each way, much longer than it took to get to my counselor job. Parking was six dollars per day (I didn't pay to park at the counselor job). The nearby lunch options were pricey. And because the days were packed, I had to spend my nights creating the daily camp schedule.

I learned that my summer gig should not be just about the salary. Granted, I was making more money, but it didn't make up for the stressful experience and added expenses. It cost me more time and more gas. I quit the director job and got my counselor job back.

Do the research. Have a conversation with a potential coworker. Ask these questions to the person who interviews you or reflect on them independently:

o How many hours will I be expected to work on the job?

o Will there be any take-home work?

o Are there any extra costs, such as parking, that I'll be expected to pay?

o Are there any special benefits offered (free gym membership, 50 percent off food purchases, and so on)?

Work from Home

You don't have to drive to work in the summertime. So long as you have a laptop, you can work from your living room couch or just about anywhere you feel comfortable. Here's a convenient way to do it: Sell your ideas. Take your personalized school resources—lesson plans and student materials—and sell them to other teachers online. You might already know about a major platform for doing this: teacherspayteachers.com (TPT). Here, teachers sell easy-to-use lesson plans from a variety of school subjects to other teachers looking for fresh ideas.

With just a little work on your days off, you can make money year-round, every time a teacher purchases a lesson plan or resource you've posted to the site. Every time! This could be a few extra hundred dollars or maybe even a few thousand.

Your best lessons will likely get the most interest. Which ones did students really rave about? And which ones received praise from your principal or other teachers? Pick out resources that stood out to you and others and see if they sell.

If you're unsure about what to sell, start by studying the site's best sellers. You can click on the best-seller list on TPT, based on your subject area and grade level. Check out the free products or even buy a few. Take note of the trendy titles, buzzwords, colors, graphics, and content.

My favorite seller is Mr. Educator. He doesn't sell just worksheets. He puts a purple cow (as mentioned in chapter 12) in all of his curriculum. He turned a lesson about the Lost Colony of Roanoke into a CIA investigation. And he also has a Declaration of Independence scavenger hunt. He's a middle school teacher in Ohio with almost 4,000 teachers subscribing to his content. You can use sellers such as Mr. Educator for inspiration as you try to figure out your own marketability.

Whether it's inside or outside the home, you can add a little to the piggy bank if you work for just a few weeks each summer. If you want to boost your income but don't want to give up your summer break, the next chapter highlights an alternative—working a side job on weeknights or weekends during the academic year.

Chapter 25

Take Up a Side Hustle During the School Year

When I think of ingenuity and hard work, I think of Nick Wilde, the sly fox from the blockbuster movie *Zootopia*. There's a scene early in the movie where he shows off his resourcefulness. Nick walks into a dessert shop and buys a gigantic, ruby-red jumbo pop for fifteen dollars. Later, he melts the popsicle and refreezes it into several smaller popsicles, which he sells to a group of lemmings, making a tidy profit. And, to top it off, Nick collects the used popsicle sticks from the lemmings and sells the sticks to a construction worker rat, who gladly buys them as building material.

But Judy Hopps, a rookie bunny cop, witnesses the whole thing. She approaches Nick to call him out for what he has done. His response: "It's called a hustle, sweetheart." Okay, let's overlook the moral and legal ramifications of Nick's side job and zoom in on a different trait: resourcefulness. He mass-produced a product at a very low cost, found a market where the product was desired, and even recycled the leftovers to increase his revenue. Selling popsicles, even though it was a sticky business, was a smart way for him to increase his income. But is it okay for teachers to work a side hustle?

> You already get your passion fix from teaching. But if you can find a side job you like, well, that's an added bonus.

Side Hustles for Teachers

For teachers, it should be legal and legit, of course. With that in mind, a side hustle is a great strategy for making money during the school year. By working part-time on school nights or during the weekends, you can create a cushion in your bank account. Like Nick's side gig, it's all about taking advantage of an opportunity to be resourceful (but in a more ethical fashion). Here are several options:

- waiting tables
- selling antiques online
- fixing computers
- house sitting
- babysitting
- tutoring
- taking photos
- delivering pizzas
- blogging
- bartending

- deejaying
- ridesharing service
- gardening and lawn care
- personal training
- cleaning houses
- event planning
- baking
- catering
- dog walking
- painting

I work two side hustles—writing and public speaking. I enjoy doing both, but I have to sacrifice some of my free time writing, reading, creating resources, and traveling to various school districts. I dabble with prep work during winter, spring, and summer break from school, I commit to speaking once every month or two, and I write for a few minutes at night or in the mornings when I can.

It isn't always easy, but the payoff makes it worth my while. I've been able to increase my annual salary by almost 20 percent. Think about what you could do with an extra 20 percent this school year. Your side hustle doesn't have to be in a field you're crazy about. You already get your passion fix from teaching. But if you can find a side job you like, well, that's an added bonus. Ultimately, what really matters is that you will have more to work with when you are off the clock. Don't be afraid to roll up your sleeves and do the dirty work.

The Rising Sun

When I opened the Teaching Fellows Scholarship letter from my mailbox my senior year in high school, I was so pumped to get into teaching. I was going to do something big with my life. But sometime between then and 2015, I lost my way. My passion disappeared. I went from loving school to despising it. I felt hopeless.

When I checked into rehab, it seemed like my world was falling apart. Honestly, it felt like the end. I didn't know in that moment, but it wasn't the end. It was the end of the Perfect Teacher Path, but it was also a new beginning.

The Rising Sun

Have you heard about the battle that took place shortly after the American Revolutionary War? It wasn't a war of guns and bullets but of ideas. What should the new government look like? This was the central question that United States leaders debated and struggled with for years. They argued long and hard over the laws that should govern the new country.

The first attempt to create laws, the Articles of Confederation, was a monumental failure: there was no executive or judicial branch of government to enforce the laws, there were no powers to tax or raise a national army, and there was no federal currency. After a few years of turmoil, representatives from each state went back to the drawing board to create a stronger federal government. They gathered together in Philadelphia for the Constitutional Convention of 1787. With James Madison at the helm as the president of the Convention, the representatives argued and debated aggressively, from May to September, on the structure and scope of government, on the rights and responsibilities of citizens within our democracy. The end result? A compromise. The United States Constitution created a strong federal government with three branches and the Bill of Rights, a powerful promise for the American people.

When the hostile debates and ratification were finally over, Benjamin Franklin asked to speak. He was seated near the back wall of the room. I can visualize him struggling as he slowly rose from his chair (he was eighty-one years old at this point) to address the young, ambitious crowd in front of him. He began by pointing to the front of the room at James Madison's chair. At the top of the convention president's seat was an etching of a sun with a few rays surrounding it. He said, "I have often . . . in the course of the session . . . looked at that sun behind the president without being able to tell whether it was rising or setting. But now, at length, I have the happiness to know it is a rising and not a setting sun."

Because of the setbacks and tension throughout the Convention, Franklin wondered if our new country was quickly coming to an end. But when the leaders finally came to a compromise and committed to the Constitution, he realized it wasn't an ending; our great country was just beginning to shine. He was right. There is no perfect country, but look how far the United States has come since we started over 200 years ago. The struggle wasn't an end. It was the beginning of something much bigger and better.

Whether you are a seasoned teacher or a new one, I'm willing to bet that the struggle has been very real for you, too. Maybe you started your career with a special passion, a belief that you would change the world, but you lost that fire. Or maybe you are at a point where you see just how much you have been letting down your spouse or how you haven't been the devoted friend you once were. Maybe your health is being compromised.

Maybe you're contemplating whether your sun is rising or setting as a teacher, whether you can keep your passion, whether you can teach and still be happy. Only you can figure out for sure where you're at. As you consider your own sun, I can only recommend you ask yourself this question: is this really an ending for me or the beginning of something new?

Sure, your first-go was a tough one, but you can learn some valuable lessons from the experience. The greatest lesson I learned is this: Being good to yourself is the best way to be good to your friends, family, and students.

Being good to yourself and to others isn't mutually exclusive. You don't have to choose one over the others. They're all available. You can have them all. You deserve to have them all. It's an unalienable right for all teachers.

Since that dark week of rehab in 2015, my sun has been rising. I'm still teaching. My school has grown quite a bit (it's now the largest middle school in North Carolina), so my classroom was moved to a mobile unit in the trailer park behind the main building. Some might see a dirty, dusty trailer, but I see a room where I can control my own AC, with a front-row view of the forest behind the school.

I'm working out three to four days each week, eating healthier, and sleeping better. I don't need prescription pills to function anymore. Several debts have been paid, and I'm saving more and building up my retirement portfolio. I'm playing basketball and reading with my son every night now. My wife and I attended monthly counseling for a while to work through our differences and get back on track. Our marriage is stronger than it's been in a long time.

Even though I felt like my world was coming to an end when I checked into rehab, my wife gave birth to a promising sign for our future, just a few weeks after I got out: a beautiful baby girl, Savannah Belle Ashley. She only weighed five pounds, but she taught me a large lesson: An ending doesn't have to be just an end. It can be a beginning. Something beautiful. The start of a newer, better you.

If you want to break free financially, you can do it. If you want to restore a relationship, you can build it. If you want a fresh bill of health, you can get it. If you want to rediscover your passion for teaching, you can find it.

The sun is rising for you, my friend. I see it. I believe it. I hope you do, too.

Weekend Plan

Time	Activity
Friday night	
Saturday morning	
Saturday afternoon	
Saturday night	
Sunday morning	
Sunday afternoon	

Song Lyric Remix Creator

Listen to "Rights Rights Baby" on YouTube for an example.

Vocabulary	Old Song Lyrics	New Song Lyrics
○ 1st Amendment ○ Bill of Rights ○ freedom of speech ○ freedom of religion ○ freedom of assembly	To the extreme I rock a mic like a vandal Light up a stage and wax a chump like a candle	To the extreme right 1's hotter than a candle Freedom to speak, believe religion, and assemble

Step 1
In the first column, list the vocabulary words, terms, phrases you're learning in class.

Step 2
Pick your favorite song and copy the lyrics into the second column. Underline the rhyming words.

Step 3
In the third column, mash-up the vocabulary and song lyrics to create the new remix. If you are having trouble with a line or phrase, look up the underlined rhyming words in rhymezone.com. You may only be able to think of five words that rhyme, but Rhymezone can give you fifty.

Step 4
Perform the song in class or with another student in class. Bonus points for adding dance moves to your song performance.

·····▶

Song Lyric Remix Creator, continued

Old Song Title:
New Song Title:
Sources Used:

Vocabulary	Old Song Lyrics	New Song Lyrics

Family Field Trip Planner

1.	26.
2.	27.
3.	28.
4.	29.
5.	30.
6.	31.
7.	32.
8.	33.
9.	34.
10.	35.
11.	36.
12.	37.
13.	38.
14.	39.
15.	40.
16.	41.
17.	42.
18.	43.
19.	44.
20.	45.
21.	46.
22.	47.
23.	48.
24.	49.
25.	50.

References and Resources

Achor, Shawn. *The Happiness Advantage: The Seven Principles of Positive Psychology that Fuel Success and Performance at Work*. New York: Crown Business, 2010.

Anderson, Mike. *The Well-Balanced Teacher: How to Work Smarter and Stay Sane Inside the Classroom and Out*. Alexandria, VA: ASCD, 2010.

Andrews, Andy. *The Noticer: Sometimes, All a Person Needs Is a Little Perspective*. Nashville, TN: Thomas Nelson, 2009.

———. *The Traveler's Gift: Seven Decisions that Determine Personal Success*. Nashville, TN: Thomas Nelson, 2002.

Bearden, Kim. *Crash Course: The Life Lessons My Students Taught Me*. New York: Simon & Schuster Paperbacks, 2014.

Berger, Jonah. *Contagious: Why Things Catch On*. New York: Simon & Schuster, 2013.

BestSelf Co. bestself.co.

Biography.com Editors. "Helen Keller Biography." A&E Television Networks. Last modified November 30, 2016. www.biography.com/people/helen-keller-9361967#death-and-legacy.

Breaux, Annette, and Todd Whitaker. *Making Good Teaching Great: Everyday Strategies for Teaching with Impact*. Larchmont, NY: Eye on Education, 2012.

Bregman, Peter. *18 Minutes: Find Your Focus, Master Distraction, and Get the Right Things Done*. New York: Business Plus, 2011.

Chapman, Gary, and Ross Campbell. *The 5 Love Languages of Children: The Secret to Loving Children Effectively*. Chicago, IL: Northfield Publishing, 2012.

Clark, Ron. *The End of Molasses Classes: Getting Our Kids Unstuck—101 Extraordinary Solutions for Parents and Teachers*. New York: Touchstone, 2011.

Covey, Stephen R. *The 7 Habits of Highly Effective People: Restoring the Character Ethic*. New York: Simon & Schuster, 1989.

Csikszentmihalyi, Mihaly. *Flow: The Psychology of Optimal Experience*. New York: Harper & Row, 1990.

Dave Ramsey. daveramsey.com.

Diamond, Dan. "Just 8% of People Achieve Their New Year's Resolutions. Here's How They Do It." *Forbes*, January 1, 2013. www.forbes.com/sites /dandiamond/2013/01/01/just-8-of-people-achieve-their-new-years-resolutions-heres-how-they-did-it/#6fd17d32304c.

Dweck, Carol S. *Mindset: The New Psychology of Success*. New York: Random House, 2006.

Fake iPhone Text Generator iOS. ios.foxsash.com.

Freedom Writers. DVD. Directed by Richard LaGravenese. Hollywood, CA: Paramount Pictures, 2007.

Getkahoot.com. getkahoot.com.

Glee. "Bad Reputation." DVD. Directed by Elodie Keene. Written by Ian Brennan. Fox Broadcasting, May 4, 2010.

Godin, Seth. *Purple Cow: Transform Your Business by Being Remarkable*. New York: Portfolio, 2003.

Goldstein, Dana. *The Teacher Wars: A History of America's Most Embattled Profession*. New York: Anchor Books, 2014.

Gordon, Jon. *The Energy Bus: 10 Rules to Fuel Your Life, Work, and Team with Positive Energy*. Hoboken, NJ: John Wiley & Sons, 2007.

———. *The No Complaining Rule: Positive Ways to Deal with Negativity at Work*. Hoboken, NJ: John Wiley & Sons, 2008.

Grooms, John. "Education Budget Slasher Thom Tillis: Teachers 'Don't Care About Kids'" *Creative Loafing Charlotte*, June 6, 2011. clclt.com/theclog /archives/2011/06/06/education-budget-slasher-thom-tillis-teachers-dont-care-about-kids.

Heath, Chip, and Dan Heath. *Made to Stick: Why Some Ideas Survive and Others Die*. New York: Random House, 2008.

Intuit Mint. www.mint.com.

Kiyosaki, Robert T., with Sharon L. Lechter. *Rich Dad Poor Dad: What the Rich Teach Their Kids About Money—That the Poor and Middle Class Do Not!* New York: Warner Books, 1998.

Lepore, Jill. *The Secret History of Wonder Woman.* New York: Vintage Books, 2015.

Levine, James A. *Get Up! Why Your Chair Is Killing You and What You Can Do About It.* New York: St. Martin's Press, 2014.

Martin, Ben. "In-Depth: Cognitive Behavioral Therapy." Psych Central. Last modified July 17, 2016. psychcentral.com/lib/in-depth-cognitive-behavioral-therapy.

Maxwell, John C. *Failing Forward: Turning Mistakes into Stepping Stones for Success.* Nashville, TN: Thomas Nelson, 2000.

McDowell, Josh. "Rules without Relationships Lead to Rebellion." Josh McDowell Ministry video, 2:27. November 16, 2010. www.youtube.com /watch?v=Tx1SOiawASw.

Moulthrop, Daniel, Nínive Clements Calegari, and Dave Eggers. *Teachers Have It Easy: The Big Sacrifices and Small Salaries of America's Teachers.* New York: The New Press, 2005.

Osteen, Joel. *Every Day a Friday: How to Be Happier 7 Days a Week.* New York: FaithWords, 2011.

PEAK Learning Systems. www.peaklearningsystems.com.

PowToon. www.powtoon.com.

Ramsey, Dave. *The Total Money Makeover: A Proven Plan for Financial Fitness.* Nashville, TN: Thomas Nelson, 2007.

Rath, Tom. *Eat Move Sleep: How Small Choices Lead to Big Changes.* Arlington, VA: Missionday, 2013.

Rath, Tom, and Jim Harter. *Wellbeing: The Five Essential Elements.* New York: Gallup Press, 2010.

Recite.com. www.recite.com.

Robinson, Ken, with Lou Aronica. *The Element: How Finding Your Passion Changes Everything.* New York: Penguin Books, 2009.

Shimoff, Marci, with Carol Kline. *Happy for No Reason: 7 Steps to Being Happy from the Inside Out.* New York: Free Press, 2008.

Sleep Cycle Alarm Clock. www.sleepcycle.com.

"Software Library: MS-DOS Games." Internet Archive. archive.org/details /softwarelibrary_msdos_games.

Stone, Douglas, and Sheila Heen. *Thanks for the Feedback: The Science and Art of Receiving Feedback Well *Even When It Is Off Base, Unfair, Poorly Delivered, and, Frankly, You're Not in the Mood.* New York: Penguin Books, 2014.

Symbaloo. www.symbaloo.com.

Teachers Pay Teachers (TPT). www.teacherspayteachers.com.

The University of Groningen. "Benjamin Franklin's Rising Sun." American History from Revolution to Reconstruction and Beyond. Accessed November 30, 2016. www.let.rug.nl/usa/outlines/government-1991/topics /benjamin-franklins-rising-sun.php.

Vanderkam, Laura. *What the Most Successful People Do on the Weekend: A Short Guide to Making the Most of Your Days Off.* New York: Portfolio/Penguin, 2012.

Watson, Angela. *Unshakeable: 20 Ways to Enjoy Teaching Every Day . . . No Matter What.* New York: Due Season Press and Educational Services, 2015.

Zootopia. DVD. Directed by Byron Howard, Rich Moore, and Jared Bush. Burbank, CA: Walt Disney Animation Studios, 2016

Index

About the Author

Justin Ashley is an award-winning teacher, motivational speaker, author, and public education advocate from Charlotte, North Carolina, where he began teaching in 2007. He is also a highly sought-after speaker for professional development. He has been an inspirational keynote presenter for thousands of current and future teachers, creating an atmosphere that bounces back and forth between rapt silence and raucous laughter. In 2013, he became the only teacher ever to win both North Carolina History Teacher of the Year and North Carolina Social Studies Teacher of the Year in the same year.

More Great Products from Free Spirit